T0129845

# THE REALITY OF
# HEAVEN

DR. JOHN THOMAS WYLIE

authorHOUSE®

AuthorHouse™
1663 Liberty Drive
Bloomington, IN 47403
www.authorhouse.com
Phone: 1 (800) 839-8640

Published by AuthorHouse 01/11/2019

ISBN: 978-1-5462-7565-7 (sc)
ISBN: 978-1-5462-7564-0 (e)

# CONTENTS

# INTRODUCTION

At some point back, it struck me my next significant stop would be "Heaven." I have turned out to be increasingly concerned about "Heaven" my future home. I started to examine the theme of "Heaven" for individual concerns. As I thought of the theme: the reality of "Heaven," I have asked a few people what they contemplated about the reality of heaven, but they appeared to sway away or offer no comments, not really wanting to hear or elaborate on the topic of heaven. I have tired to find books regarding the matter in the best book shops, but my findings did not satisfy my inward longings. It is here that I take up my pen in perspective of its importance for each believer.

We live in a materialistic and cash situated world where the subject of "Heaven" has apparently been consigned to the back burner. It is only here and there examined or rarely find a place in present day media.

In any case, In on resolute faith in the total motivation and final authority of the Bible, it doesn't disclose to every one of us all we might want to know concerning heaven, but the Bible reveals all we have to know.

There are numerous topics identifying with heaven that are not talked about here, and for them the reader can reference the most exhaustive treatments. Despite the fact that this blocks a reliably, continuous advancement regarding the matter, it might be increasingly useful from a practical perspective. Because the very Reality of heaven arouses so many questions in one's mind, I have adopted a question-and-answer format as well as an informative format.

I Trust this publication, "The Reality Of Heaven," will touch your spirit and mind as you read. Philippians 1:21-23 reads: "For me to live is Christ, and to die is gain." "But if I live in the flesh, this is the fruit of my labour; yet what I shall choose I wot not." "For I am in a strait betwixt two, having a desire to depart, and to be with Christ; which is far better."

There is each explanation behind the believer to anticipate the future with glad expectation, regardless of whether for the person in question it holds the second appearance of the Lord, or entering through entryways of our "heavenly home" by way of death. This isn't negligible pie in the sky considering, however all around established certainty.

We may impart to Paul's conviction that to be with Christ is obviously better than anything we can imagine. The personal satisfaction and service here has an undeniable bearing on our felicity and reward there.

Reverend Dr. John Thomas Wylie

# CHAPTER

# ONE

◇◇◇◇◇

# Definition Of Heaven

"The English translation of several Hebrew and Greek words. The emphasis in some of these is "height;" hence, heaven is something above. The term is applied to the firmament, which is spread out like an arch above the earth. Sometimes, it is used with "earth" to denote the whole universe (Gen. 1:1); also it is used to denote the "sky", the place where the sun, moon and stars dwell (Ezk. 32:7, Matt. 24:29, 16:1);it is also used of the regions above the sky the location of things eternal and perfect, where God and other heavenly beings dwell (Matt. 5:34, 23:22)."

"This is probably what Paul referred to as the "third heaven" (II Cor. 12:2). Scripture does not specifically describe the first and second heavens; some view the first as the atmosphere, the second as the spaces where supernatural beings dwell, and the third is the abode of God. It is a place (II Cor. 12:2, John 14:1-3) of glory and beauty (Rev.21:1-22:7) (The New Combined Bible Dictionary And Concordance, 1984)."

◇◇◇◇◇

# Heaven Is Both A Place And A State

That Heaven is a condition of endless blessedness is conceded by all. Be that as it may, heaven is a place too. In our dialog of the Intermediate State we pointed the scriptural training that both heaven and Hell are places, and the at death, souls enter the one or the other. There they hold up the judgment which will settle their last state with its rewards or punishments.

Heaven, in this way, as we should now see it, is the home the saved in their last condition of glorification. It is maybe difficult to discuss in reference to spiritual bodies, in a similar sense that we utilize the term when talking about the present assortments of fragile living flesh and blood. We know, be that as it may, that Jesus helped His grieving disciples with the words, In My Father's home are numerous chateaus; if it were not really so, I would have let you know. I go to prepare a place for you. Furthermore, in the event that I go and prepare a place for you, I will return once more, and receive you unto myself; that where I am, there ye may be also (John 14:2,3).

Be that as it may, we require not here examine the connection of the spiritual body to space. The Scriptures talk about the physical sky above us, however they likewise discuss a third heaven, where God abides and where His glory is showed in a particularly unbelievable sense.

Paul talks about being made up for lost time in the most astounding heaven whether in the body or out of the body, he couldn't tell, and having heard there, words which couldn't be expressed. It is regularly assumed this was the event when he saw the glorified body of Jesus (I Cor. 9:1).

Stephen looked relentlessly into heaven, and saw the glory of God, and Jesus standing on the right hand of God (Acts 7:55); and Paul discloses to us that to be missing from the body is to be present with the Lord (II Cor. 5:8).

We require not, hence, think about the spirit as voyaging long separations spatially, so as to enter heaven. The separation isn't to be considered as far as physical space, however of changed conditions. At the rising Jesus was taken up into heaven, and a cloud received Him out of sight (Acts 1:9).

Heaven, accordingly, is simply behind the cloak (veil), which so regularly yet "thinly intervenes," as denoting what to us is visible, and that which is past the scope of mortal sight. The word end of the world means a revealing, and at death, the righteous go through this shroud (veil) into the blissful vision of Christ.

This to the redeemed soul is heaven. In any case, as the cloud veiled Jesus from the sight of the disciples, so likewise, He will come back again with clouds, that is, He will blast through the veil at the end of the world, and be uncovered from heaven in majesty, glory and power.

Whenever likewise, Paul discusses Jesus as having ascended up far above the heavens, that he might fill all things (Eph. 4:10), he isn't speaking essentially of physical distance, but of his wonderful majesty, glory and the fullness of His redeeming grace. Heaven, subsequently, will be a place, the eternal abode of all the redeemed of all ages.

John states explicitly, that he saw the holy city, new Jerusalem, descending from God out of heaven, prepared as a bride of the hour adorned for her husband (Rev. 21:2); and once more, he heard the words, Come hither, I will show thee the bride, the Lamb's wife (Rev. 21:9).

John Miley puts it this way: "The Scriptures ever represent heaven as a place. This is so plain a fact that it hardly needs any illustration. Our Lord represented it as a place or mansion in His Father's house (John 14:1-3); Paul as a building of God, a house not made with hands, eternal in the heavens (II Cor. 5:1)."

"Again, it is the temple of God, the place of His throne and glory (Rev. 7:9-17); and a great city, the holy Jerusalem (Rev. 21:10). No doubt these are figurative representations of heaven; but that does not affect the underlying reality of place." (Miley, Systematic Theology, 2009).

These references unmistakably demonstrate that the apostle is speaking about the Church in her consummated wonder, her perfected glory. Other passages, be that as it may, appear to allude to the Church militant on earth. Along these lines, they will bring the glory and honour of the nations into it (Rev. 21:26).

One passage appears to blend the militant and triumphant aspects of the Church in a solitary explanation (a single statement) - And the nations of them which are saved will walk in the light of it, alluding to the light which streams down from the Jerusalem which is above; and the kings of the earth do bring their glory and honour into it - alluding to the Church Militant on earth (Rev. 21:24).

Dr. Adam Clarke (1912) makes a significant remark: "There is a blessed state beyond this life, of which we cannot speak minutely as if we had seen it, but of which we can speak confidently because we know the principle of it. The man who has entered it is present with God and with Christ, in a clearer and truer consciousness of the divine presence than was possible on earth, and enters upon the higher stages of that divine life which has already been begun. He is living the life of progressive holiness; he is like his Lord and Saviour, and is ever growing more like Him, advancing to perfection."

"He is under the most holy and inspiring influences, where all that is best in him is constantly helped to increase. All characteristic activities of the Christlike life are open to him. The grade of being in which he finds himself higher than that which he has left, and fresh opportunities of holy service and of holy growth and blessedness are constantly set before him. He is in the life that he loves and ought to love, and the course of free and Godlike activity stretches on before him without end (W. N. Clarke, 1912, An Outline Of Christian Theology)."

The statement Clarke shows above as demonstrating the snappy change in thought from the Church activist to the Church Triumphant. On Rev. 21:2 concerning the new Jerusalem he says, "This without a doubt implies the Christian Church in a state of extraordinary prosperity and purity"; while the declaraion, "there will be no more earth," he applies to the Church after the resurrection.

The genuine understanding of the last three sections of the Apocalypse is this: "In the preceding part of Revelation a prophetic portray had been given of the history of the Church to the commencement of Christ's millennial reign . In the last three chapters the millennial reign of Christ, the solemn events of the resurrection, the general judgment, and the glories of the future state, are depicted.

As the millennial reign of Christ with His Saints on earth will go before, and is commonplace of, His triumphant reign with them in the heavenly state, the most rational inference is, that both of these states are incorporated. The burden of this description verifiably relates with the heavenly state; yet, as both millennial reign of Christ, the one unfurling its most prominent triumphs in this world and the other uncovering its last issues on the world to come, it is nevertheless common that the portrayal of both ought to be blended. The triumphs of Christ's mediatorial reign on earth, and its rewards in heave, are, in an important sense, one (Ralston,1851, 2010 Elements Of Divinity).

◇◇◇◇◇

## The Blessedness Of The Saints

While the nature of future happiness can't be known in this life, the Scriptures give us numerous insinuations of what God has a prepared for them that love Him. (1) Heaven will be a place from which all transgression (sin) and wickedness will be exiled (banished) for eternity. There shall in no wise enter into it any thing that defileth, neither whatsoever worketh abomination, or maketh a lie (Rev. 21:27)

No unholy thing will ever enter the dwelling place the blessed, nor will the holy people ever feel the vile impact of Satan or mischievous men. (2) It will be a place where the penal consequences of transgression (sin) are altogether removed. And God shall wipe away all tears from their eyes; and there shall be no more death, neither sorrow, nor crying, neither shall there be any more pain; for the former things are passed away (Rev. 21:4).

(3) Heaven won't just be characterized adversely by the nonappearance of all malicious, but the holy people will likewise enjoy the possession of all positive good. The curse having been removed, John says, The throne of God and of the Lamb shall be in it; and his servants shall serve him: and they shall see his face; and his name shall be in

their foreheads. And there shall be no night there; and they need no candle, neither light of the sun; for the Lord God giveth them Light: and they shall reign for ever and ever (Rev. 22:3-5).

The Scriptures just cited represent heaven as the perfect answer of each holy desire. For the individuals who are exhausted, it is everlasting rest; for the grieving, it is where God shall wipe away all tears; for the suffering, there shall be no more suffering; for the mistakes and bumbles of a sincere but imperfect service, the throne of God shall be there, and His Servants shall serve Him-each deed being performed in His presence and under His approving smile; for the individuals who are confounded and puzzled by the vulnerabilities and frustrations of this life, it is promised that there shall be no night there; for the Lord God giveth them light, and they shall reign with Him for all eternity.

Another wellspring of blessedness to the holy people (saints), will be their fellowship with one another and with their Lord. We might make certain that the unmistakable identity of each redeemed holy person will be saved intact; and that the social impulses which described them here, won't be devastated there, but rather strengthened.

Hence the apostle says, But ye are come unto mount Sion, and unto the city of the living God, the heavenly Jerusalem, and to an innumerable company of angels, to the general assembly and church of the firstborn, which are written in heaven, and to God the Judge of all, and to the spirits of just men made perfect (Heb. 12:22, 23).

Our Lord says that they shall come from the east and west, and shall sit down with Abraham, and Isaac, and Jacob, in the kingdom of heaven (Matt. 8:11). "They shall hold converse with prophets and righteous men of olden time. They shall listen to the addresses of Enoch and Elijah, of Abraham and Job, of Moses and Samuel, of David and Isaiah, of Daniel and Ezekiel, of Peter and James, of Paul and John. If a few of moments of Mt. Tabor, where Moses and Elijah talked with Jesus, so entranced the apostles, with what thrilling emotions should the souls of the redeemed be roused, when on the everlasting mount on high they shall listen to the sublime strains in which such so many of cloquent and immortal tongues shall comment on the stupendous wonders of redemption! (Ralston, 2010, Elements Of Divinity)."

Moreover, the plain inference of sacred writing is, that the holy people will recognize and mingle with their friends and family of earth, who such as themselves have been saved through the blood of the Lamb. "Then shall I know," writes the Apostle Paul, "even as also I am known" (I Cor. 13:12).

To the inquiry, Shall we know each other in heaven? We may at that point, certainly reply in the positive. Since memory remains, and the topic of our song is redemption, we might be assured that we will likewise hold the knowledge of people, places, and conditions associated with our salvation.

Paul seems to hold out to the Thessalonians the delight of this knowledge when he says, For what is our hope, or joy, or crown of rejoicing? Are not even ye in the presence of our Lord Jesus Christ at his coming? (I Thess. 2:19).

"Heaven will be replete with loving fellowships and holy worship. The imperfections which so often mar our present social life, even in its most spiritual forms, will have no place in those fellowships. There love shall be supreme. Through the headship of Christ saints and angels shall form a happy brotherhood. Yet the saints will have a song and a joy which angels can share only by the power of sympathy – the song of redemption and the joy of salvation. Holy love will make all duty a holy delight. The heavenly worship, kindled by the immediate presence and open vision of God and the Lamb, shall be full of holy rapture (Miley, J., 2009, System Theology)."

If the apostle anticipated gathering the individuals who had been converted over under his ministry, may not all cherish a same hope in respect to their own friends and family? But, most noteworthy and best, it is promised that without dimming veil, they shall see his face; and his name shall be in their foreheads (Rev. 22:4); and John in an equally exultant strain exclaims, Beloved, now are we the sons of God, and it doth not appear what we shall be: but we know that, when he shall appear, we shall be like him; for we shall see him as he is. And every man that hath this hope in him purifieth himself, even as he is pure (I John 3:2, 3).

◇◇◇◇◇

## The Employments Of Heaven

While heaven will be a place of rest, we are not to assume that it will be a place of idleness or inactivity. The inquiry, hence, normally emerges, What will be the nature of the employments of heaven?

We may well guess that they will be as a matter of first importance profound. God, who hath blessed us with all spiritual blessings in heavenly places in Christ Jesus (Eph.

1:3), will enable the souls of the redeemed to always expand in the ocean-fullness of divine love.

He who hath redeemed them, will dwell in the midst of them, and lead them to wellsprings of living waters. New views of divine grace, and fresh visions of His adorable person, continually burst in upon their enraptured minds and hearts. Before them will lie the whole circle of creation, the system of providence and the character of God.

His Wisdom, love and power they will have the capacity to trace in the mysteries of nature and providence which are presently concealed from human eyes....The delights in the mind must make up an extraordinary part of the blessedness of heaven.

The freed and expanded reason will no doubt thoroughly enjoy following (tracing) the laws of the material universe and the supreme wisdom which ordained them, the rise and advancement of the different kingdoms and domains, countries and races, which constitute the dominion of God; in tracing the wisdom, love and goodness of the Creator in every department of being, from the creepy crawly insect on earth to the seraph before the throne. Gracious, what a field for the intellect!

Nor must we overlook the bodily enjoyments also. A new physical framework or bodily organism will be given to the soul at the resurrection, which will so perfectly express the new redeemed and spiritual nature, that it is known as a spiritual body. The soul and body were made for one another, and death which occasioned their separation in this life, will itself be annihilated, destroyed in the world to come.

◇◇◇◇◇

# The Endless Duration Of Heaven

The crowning excellency of heaven is, that its joys will never end. Heaven is designated "the city of God," a city which hath foundations, whose builder and maker is God (Heb. 11:10); it is known as a better country, that is, an heavenly (Heb. 11:16); and it is spoken of as a kingdom which can't be moved (Heb. 12:28).

The word forever (eternity) or a portion of its structures, is as often as possible related with heaven. It is a house...eternal in the heavens (II Cor. 5:1); eternal glory (I Peter 5:10); everlasting habitations (Luke 16:9); and the everlasting kingdom of our Lord and Savior Jesus Christ (II Peter 1:11). The word endlessness is utilized regarding interminable life, eternal life. Truth be told, the endlessness of things to come life is fundamental to the existence itself. The specific probability of an end would genuinely deface the idea of its felicity and security.

When the holy people (saints, the redeemed) go into that everlasting glory, they enter upon an actual existence (eternal glory) that will never be finished, and of which it might be said of them, as it is of God himself, that their "years will have no end."

A.A. Hodge,(1860, 1972) comments in his book, "Outlines of Theology," the following (Paraphased): "In mediating upon what is revealed of the conditions of heavenly existence two errors are to be avoided: (1) the extreme of regarding the mode of existence experienced by the saints in heaven as too nearly analogous to that of our earthly life; (2) the opposite extreme of regarding the conditions of the heavenly life as too widely distinguished from that of our present experience."

"The evil effect of the first extreme will, of course, be to degrade by unworthy associations our conceptions of heaven; while the evil effect of the opposite extreme will be in great measure to destroy the moral power which is a hope of heaven should naturally exert over our hearts and lives, by rendering our conception of it vague, and our sympathy with its characteristics consequently distant and feeble."

"To avoid both of these extremes, we should fix the limits within which our conceptions of the future existence of the saints must range, by distinguishing between those elements of man's nature, and of his relations to God and other men, which are essential and unchangeable, and those elements which must be changed to order to render his nature in his relations perfect."

"The following must be changed: (1) all sin and its consequences must be removed; (2) spiritual bodies must take the place of our present flesh and blood; (3) the new heavens and the new earth must take the place of the present heavens and earth as the scene of man's life; (4) the laws of social organization must be radically changed, since in heaven there will be no marriage, but a social order analogous to that of the "angels of God" introduced."

XXX "The accompanying components are fundamental, and accordingly unchangeable: (1) man will proceed with ever to exist, as aggravated of two natures, a profound and material. (2) He is basically savvy and should live by information. (3) He is basically dynamic, and must have work to do. (4) Man can, as a limited animal, know

God mediately, that is, through His works of creation and provision, the experience of His charitable work upon our souls, and through His Incarnate Son, who is the picture of His individual, and the completion of the Godhead substantial."

"God will, along these lines, in paradise keep on showing man through His works, and to follow up on him by methods for thought processes routed to his will through his comprehension. (5) The memory of man never at long last loses the smallest impression, and it will have a place with the flawlessness of the grand express that each experience gained in the past will dependably be inside the ideal control of the will.

(6) Man is basically a social being. This, taken regarding the past point, demonstrates the end that the relationship, and additionally the experience of our natural life, will convey the majority of their characteristic results with them into the new homestead presence, aside from as so far they are essentially adjusted (not lost) by the change."

(7) "Man's life is basically an interminable advancement toward limitless flawlessness. (8) All the known analogies of God's works in creation, in His fortune in the material and good world, and in His allotment of elegance, show that in paradise holy people will vary among themselves both as to innate limits and characteristics, and as to relative position and office."

These distinctions will without a doubt be resolved (a) by established contrasts of common limit, (b) by generous rewards in paradise relating in kind and degree to the benevolent productivity of the person on earth, (c) by the supreme sway of the Creator."

"Now the God of peace, that brought again from the dead our Lord Jesus, that great shepherd of the sheep, through the blood of the everlasting covenant, make you perfect in every good work to do his will, working in you that which is well pleasing in his sight, through Jesus Christ; to whom be glory for ever and ever. Amen." (Heb. 13:20-21).

# CHAPTER

# TWO

◇◇◇◇◇

# In What Sense Is Heaven "Better"?

"If I am to go on living in the body, this will mean fruitful work for me. Yet what shall I choose? I do not know! I am torn between the two: I desire to depart and be with Christ, which is better by far; but it is more necessary for you that I stay in the body (Philippians 1:22-24)."

Paul was torn between a sense of pastoral obligation and the longing for personal delight and fulfillment. He was in no doubt concerning which was better. Had he not had a foretaste of heaven? In a self-portraying reference he wrote:

'I know a man in Christ who fourteen years ago was caught up to the third heaven. Whether it was in the body or out of the body I do not know-God knows. And, I know that this man...was caught up to paradise. He heard inexpressible things, things that man is not permitted to tell. (II Corinthians 12:2-4)."

So when Paul said that heaven was better by a long shot, he was speaking from experience. When the hour of his martyrdom drew near, he faced it with a cheerful serenity and sublime assurance. There was no fear or reluctance.

"For I am already being poured out like a drink offering, and the time has come for my departure. I have fought a good fight, I have finished the race, I have kept the faith. Now there is in store for me the crown of righteousness, which the Lord, the righteous Judge, will award me on that day...(II Timothy 4:6-8)."

Early historians commented on the valor and bliss with which Christians confronted cruel death. In A.D. 125, in a letter to a companion, Aristides portrayed "another religion called "Christianity." "If any equitable man among the Christians goes from this world, they cheer, and offer because of God; and they escort the body with melodies of thanksgiving, as though he were setting out starting with one place then onto the next nearby."

Those enduring holy people accomplished a healthy and triumphant way to deal with the truth of death, since they had put stock in and encountered the power of Christ's resurrection and they esteemed a healthy certainty (faith) that a joyous heaven awaited them.

The conspicuous difference between their satisfaction and triumph and the miserable grieving and crying of their agnostic peers within the sight of death demonstrated an incredible evangelistic agency.

The truth and reality of heaven is far better than and superior to the best experiences of earth, that one can outline just a couple of its advantages and favors:

* We will appreciate everlasting life in the immediate presence of the triune God.
* All that lessens the personal satisfaction on earth will be exiled from heaven.
* The heights of joy we have encountered on earth will be eclipsed in heaven.
* We will be "saved to sin no more." Failure and its consequuences will be a relic of days gone by.
* No more will we be subject to the temptations from the world, the flesh, and the fallen angel (the devil).
* Knowledge will never again be restricted.

* Limitations of the body will hamper us no more.
* Everything that would enrich our lives will be accessible.
* Reunion with friends and family and the development of new relationships will make heaven a great place of fellowship.
* Heaven's music will far outperform earth's best or finest accomplishments in that realm.
* There will be full fulfillment or satisfaction for every holy and wholesome longing and aspiration.

What's more to desire. To put it plainly, the reality of heaven is far superior and beyond ways for which words can not describe. In Brief, Heaven is Far Better! This problem now is that with our finite minds, we cannot imagine it.

◇◇◇◇◇

## Is There Life After Death?

"If a man dies, will he live again?" (Job 14:14)

Despite Paul's certain affirmation to the followers at Philippi-and to us-that "For to me, to live is Christ and to die is gain" (Philippians 1:21), and that "to depart and be with Christ...is far better" (Philippians 1:23), even among Christians there is an across the board fear of the desolate involvement of death.

Or then again maybe it might be fear of the process of dying as opposed to fear of death itself. There are numerous encounters in life that are inside our control, yet this is something that is inescapable and escapes our grip.

Yet, death still remains death and is a point of discussion stayed away from studiously by many.

To the inquiry, If a man dies, will he live again? There are distinctive answers from various groups. The rationalist, when confronting death, may state, I am bringing a dreadful jump into the dark. The materialist may state, I see nothing more in individuals than insignificant fragile living flesh and blood. They originate from earth and come back to earth. They have no future.

Scientists can toss no light on the issue, nor should we anticipate that they should, for science bargains just with things that can be seen with our faculties. Of things past experience science knows nothing legitimate. The skeptic or the agnostic does not have faith in any divine disclosure and keeps up that nobody knows or can comprehend what lies past death.

Among people both agnostic and refined there is an innate want for "everlasting status-immortality". Proof of this natural yearning is available among most crude people groups, just like a confidence in presence after death. While these thoughts are not really a proof of certain survival, they are proof of a relatively all inclusive faith in "everlasting status -immortality" that must be accounted for.

One basic element of these ideas is that they conceive this present life as proceeding inconclusively after death, together with the delight of every single physical desire. Another normal idea among numerous groups is that in the following life there will be reward for virtue, compensation for suffering, and punishment for bad behavior. Is this universal desire and conviction simply an illusion, or does it have its roots in reality?

Some see this inquiry as unimportant in space age, or in the age of the internet. The possibility of an actual existence endless euphoria after death is viewed as doubtful and strange. Sitting on a cloud strumming a brilliant harp is definitely not appealing prospect. Indeed, even among a few Christians, the mainstream good news of "well-being, riches, and achievement" in this life has served to diminish any longing for heaven. Heaven can be here and now.

Be that as it may, faith in post-existence is inborn in mankind's exceptionally constitution, for God "has also set time eternity in the hearts of men" (Ecclesiastes 3:11).

The hope of life after death and related topics was conspicuous in both discussion and writing a century prior, but today the without further ado so engages the consideration of the vast majority that "immortality" isn't in their vocabularies.

Heaven and hell have turned out to be progressively uncommon notes in contemporary preaching, and this is reflected in the popular attitude.

There has, be that as it may, as of late been slight inversion of this pattern, maybe as a spin off from the commonness of wrongdoing, crime, brutality, and wars in our society. The ubiquity of Eastern religions and the quick increment in mysterious action (occult) have additionally invigorated enthusiasm for this area.

Likewise, interest has been excited in the once in the past doubtful by the broad cases of individuals who had been classed as clinically dead but were breathed life back into, that they had upbeat "out-of-body" encounters while "dead."

Among the Greek rationalists who contended for the

indestructibility of the spirit, Cicero asserted that there is in the brain of individuals a specific presentiment of immortality, which takes the most profound root and is most discoverable in the greatest geniuses and the most exalted souls.

When to this weight of extra-biblical proof for "immortality" is included the unmistakable and unequivocal statements of the trustworthy Word of God, we can confirm with certainty that there is in fact life after death.

At the point when Harriet Beecher Stowe, creator of the outstanding "Uncle Tom's Cabin," was confronted with her beyond a reasonable doubt her dearly loved son Henry's death, she stated, "Jesus will give me back my loved one whom He is educating in a far higher sphere than I proposed."

◇◇◇◇◇

## Death: Enemy Or Benefactor?

"O death, where is thy sting? O grave, where is thy victory? The sting of death is sin…."(I Corinthians 15:55, 56)

This optimistic verse grasps two of the most disliked words in the English dialect - "death and grave." Paul has as a main priority the deadly and unbearably difficult sting of the scorpion, which he compares with wrongdoing in its agonizing outcomes. Despite the fact that the instrumentality of wrongdoing, death and the grave have for centuries held barbarous influence over humankind.

The author of the letters to the Hebrews alludes to "the

those who all their lives were held in slavery by their fear of death" (Hebrews 2:15).

In the amazing questioning of I Corinthians 15, Paul contends that in His resurrection, Christ extracted death's sting and victimized the grave of its transient triumph. Indeed, even before His resurrection Jesus ruined the funerals He visited.

The grave's triumph was turned around, and death's sting neutralized. When Jesus rose from the dead, Satan experienced a fantastic annihilation which he will never recuperate.

The powerful passage cited above tosses down a twofold test to death and the grave. Since the resurrection of Christ, no Christian has any reason for fearing the changes death may bring. Where is now the anonymous fear that has frequented the hearts of people since that fateful day in Eden?

◇◇◇◇◇

## What Is Death Anyway?

How may it be characterized? In an lecture revealed in the London Times of December 12, 1967, Dr. H. Beecher proposed three accommodating medicinal definitions:

Passing Occurs:

1.  The minute at which irreversible pulverization of mind matter, with no probability of recovering cognizance, is indisputably decided.

2. The minute at which unconstrained heartbeat can't be reestablished.
3. The occasion "mind passing" is built up by the electroencephalogram.

Maybe the easiest definition from the religious perspective is "partition from the wellspring of life."

The Scriptures separates three sorts of death:

Physical - the division of the body from the spirit and soul.
Otherworldly - the detachment of soul and soul from God.
Endless - profound demise made perpetual. "This is the second demise" (Rev. 21:8).

However, Jesus taught His disciples that, for a believer, the end of life isn't "death." He saved that magnificent word for a significance of vastly more profound import and demanded calling the death of a believer "sleep."

"Before going to the tomb of Lazarus He said to His disciples,

"Our friend Lazarus has fallen asleep; but I am going there to wake him up."

"His disciples replied, "Lord, if he sleeps, he will get better." Jesus had been speaking of his death, but his disciples thought he meant natural sleep."

So then he told them plainly, "Lazarus is dead..." (John 11:11-14).

The supporters were cold-hearted in not understanding that He was not discussing rest in physical sleep; but rather since they endured in their misinterpretation, Jesus place it in plain dialect.

A Preacher once stated, "Jesus accomplished more than sleep." "Christ died for our transgressions." (I Corinthians 15:3). On Calvary He encountered the physical suspension we term death. Be that as it may, for Him, with respect to no other, death held immense and deplorable ramifications. A significant number of His followers persevered through the horrendous enduring of torturous killing (the crucifixion) as He did. In any case, they didn't die. They just slept.

The misery and anguish of the cross, the devastation emerging from being spurned, or forsaken by His Father, the devastating burden of a world's wrongdoing (sin) this was death the repulsiveness of dark haziness, the midnight of the spirit . Jesus died all together that believers may "sleep".

Understanding this ought to exile the dread of death, the one experience over which we have no control. To some, be that as it may, it isn't so much dying's murkiness they fear, but the way toward death, and what might be ahead after that. For them, this is the aggravating component.

In prior years it was in the home that births and death occurred. They were simply part of typical family life and were acknowledged accordingly. These occasions were the ordinary subjects of discussion.

Presently they occur, not in the home but rather in the hospital or medical center. Presently these cozy family happenings are segregated to the point that numerous people have no understanding of contact with death and dying until midlife. These things are in this manner remote from reality, and that makes the unmistakable reality increasingly hard to confront when it comes. Dying has turned into an inadmissible subject of numerous discussions.

Notwithstanding, death ought not be seen as an end but rather as a passage driving into an ampler and amazingly increasingly superb and wonderful world. The dying of an adherent (believer) is a change, not a last condition. It is useful to remember that it is just the natural body that is unfavorably influenced by death.

The individuals who confront dying most unhesitatingly have completely acknowledged its certainty and have an essential faith in Jesus Christ. They can confront that inevitability with a scripturally based affirmation of their own salvation.

All through Scripture, dying is spoken to as the final product of sin . So Paul is right in depicting it as the last adversary to be obliterated. The early church shared his perspective and came to view death as a crushed adversary and, consequently, as a promoter who would present on them a boundless help. "With Jesus Christ, and The Reality of Heaven So much Better by far!"

# CHAPTER

# THREE

◇◇◇◇◇

# A Place Or A State?

Although we have discussed whether the reality of heaven is a place or state in chapter one we shall discuss it again briefly in somewhat a different perspective. For this is a paramount question concerning life after death. We shall revisit the topic again. Will we know one another in heaven?

"...many will come from the east and the west, and will take their places at the feast with Abraham, Isaac, and Jacob..." (Matthew 8:11).

To many, this is the central inquiry concerning eternal life. Vulnerability with regards to the appropriate response has obfuscated the expectation of paradise for a few. It would be no happy place for them if that they were not able perceive companions and friends and family of the earthly past. One of the expectant joys of heaven is the prospect of reunion.

The plan to see each other in heaven is totally characteristic, really human and in congruity with the Scriptures. Life in heaven will bring advancement, not impoverishment.

There is no Scripture entry that proposes the abrogation of every previous relationship when we land in heaven.

It is the fundamental component of identity that will persevere after death, not the impermanent "tent" in which it is housed on this earth. The body is bound to come back to dust, but the internal man, the soul, lives on, and its identity with the body isn't broken, nor breached.

Heavenly attendants have no bodies, but then they exist

and go about as unmistakable identities. In the event that holy messengers who have no bodies can remember each other, for what reason should this not be true or possible for believers?

In Daniel 9:21 and 10:13 it is recorded that Michael the lead heavenly host provided to the with some much needed help of his partner Gabriel, when the last was frustrated in his main goal by satanic offices. If angels, why not men and women?

The rebuilding of sundered connections is unmistakably imagined in I Thessalonians 4:15-17.

"...we who are still alive, who are left till the coming of the Lord, will certainly not precede those who have fallen asleep. For the Lord himself will come down from heaven, with a loud command, with the voice of the archangel and with the trumpet call of God, and the dead in Christ will rise first. After that, we who are still alive and are left will be caught up together with them in the clouds to meet the Lord in the air. And so we will be with the Lord forever."

If there were no recognition in heaven, would not our Lord's illustration about the rich man and Lazarus in Luke 16 be without importance?

"And in the parable of the dishonest steward, Jesus said to His disciples, "I tell you, use worldly wealth to gain friends for yourselves, so that when it is gone, you will be welcomed into eternal dwellings" (Luke16:9)."

Jesus here imagined His disciples being invited into paradise by the individuals who had been the recipients of their liberality when on earth. Gold put resources into God's work is transmuted into souls won to Christ and workers provided for His service.

Paul foreseen the joy that would be his when he met in heaven those whom he had been privileged to lead to saving faith in Christ. "For what is our hope, our joy, or the crown in which we will glory in the presence of our Lord Jesus when he comes? Is it not you?" (I Thess. 2:19).

That passage surely certainly implies joyous recognition. And there are other biblical instances of reunion and recognition. At the garden tomb, Mary at first did not know Jesus after His resurrection and confused Him with the gardener. Be that as it may, when she heard the dearest voice saying "Mary!" "she moved in the direction of Him and shouted out in Aramaic, 'Rabboni!'" (which implies Teacher)" (John 20:16). His manner of speaking was promptly unmistakable.

So no doubt the heavenly and spiritual connections of life on earth won't be disjoined, however will proceed in purified frame. Family connections among believers won't be broken. Dying won't crush our association with the past.

Obviously the most grounded contention for the acknowledgment of friends and family in paradise is simply the presence of our Lord in His resurrection body, when He said to His disciples, "It is I myself! Touch me and see; a ghost does not have flesh and bones, as you see I have" (Luke 24:39).

Is heaven a place or a state of mind? "Do not let your hearts be troubled. Trust in God; trust also in me. In my Father's house are many mansions; if it were not so, I would have told you. I am going to prepare a place for you. And if I go and prepare a place for you, I will come back and take you to be with me that you also may be where I am." (John 14:1-3).

We experience challenges the minute we attempt to depict in our space-time dialect occasions and conditions that are past reality. In the book of Revelation John is attempting to express inconceivable, endless things in the main vehicle accessible to him. That is the reason, under the direction of the Holy Spirit, he utilized blemished natural terms to depict a magnificent place.

At the point when Paul endeavored to portray his "third paradise" encounter, he met a similar issue. He could state only that he "heard inconceivable things, things that man isn't permitted to tell" (II Cor. 12:4).

Since this is along these lines, we can't translate representative writing in a woodenly exacting and unoriginal way, as we would a logical treatise. Nor should we fall into the contrary mistake of undue spiritualization of the content. Doors of pearl and roads of gold are obviously allegorical and ought to be so translated, but they do represent something genuine and considerable.

Heaven is a state in an area some place in the great universe of God. It's anything but a material place that we can situate from down here. The main piece of information we have as to its whereabouts was given by Jesus when He said to the disciples, "I will return and take you to be with me that you also might be in the place I am" (John 14:3). Heaven is accordingly where God is.

Heaven isn't in a spatial sense, however the dialect utilized passes on the possibility that it is boundlessly higher than all that we know. In His humankind, Jesus could uncover this grand truth to individuals just in wording that we could get it.

All in all, the inquiry is, Is Heaven a place? The

appropriate response is, Yes, and No. It's anything but a place in the material sense in which, state, Jerusalem is a place. It will be on a very basic level unique in relation to our present, space-time condition. To Jesus, paradise was the place His Father has His home.

Yet, even this establishes an issue, for "God is Spirit" (John 4:24). Along these lines He doesn't possess space as we probably am aware of it. He has no substantial shape. Would this not suggest that heaven is a state as opposed to a place?

We, nonetheless, are not spirit as the Father seems to be. We will have spiritual bodies. Jesus, as well, keeps on having His resurrection body, which is some place. This would appear to require area.

In the Lord's Prayer there is the appeal, "your will be done on earth for what it is in heaven" (Matt. 6:10). This, as well, would propose that heaven has a region, as does the earth (Luke 15:7).

The Ascension of Christ, at that point, proposes that heaven is a genuine place. He went some place, yet the main manner by which this place can be portrayed is by the guide of scriptural images. While heaven isn't a real city, it resembles a city. Everything we can say with confirmation is the thing that the Bible says it resembles and what antagonistic natural highlights will be absent from it.

◇◇◇◇◇

# Can The Living Communicate With The Dead?

"When men instruct you to counsel mediums and spiritists, who murmur, whisper and mumble, ought not a people ask of their God? Why consult the dead on behalf of the living?" (Isaiah 8:19)

It is conceivable to lift the window ornament that isolates the living from the dead? Would we be able to speak with the individuals who have died? These are questions that emerge, particularly in the minds of the individuals who have cherished profoundly and are currently dispossessed. They long for some solace in the domain of the supernatural.

One of the evil impacts of war and across the board catastrophic events is a recrudescence of spiritism-the endeavor to hold correspondence with the spirits of the dead through the office of extraordinarily defenseless mediums.

In a period of emergency, when a home has a vacant seat, such an improvement is effectively comprehended. Is the cherished one happy? Is it true that he is or she aware of what is happening on earth? Be that as it may, the act of spiritism is completely "condemned" in Scripture and is "entirely and strictly forbidden."

"Let no one be found among you...who practices divination or sorcery, interprets omens, engages in witchcraft, or casts spells, or who is a medium or a spiritist or who consults the dead. Anyone who does these things is destestable to the Lord" (Deut. 18:10-12).

The New Testament is no less vocal in its "warning" than the Old. The ascent of present day spiritism is one of the anticipated indications of the most recent days, concerning which express "warning" is given the "Holy Spirit of God:"

"The Holy Spirit clearly says that in latter times some will abandon the faith and follow deceiving spirits and things taught by demons. Such teachings come through hypocritical liars, whose consciences have been seared as with a hot iron" (I Tim. 4:1-2).

A few analysts (commentators) have depicted the Old Testament legends (heroes) deified in Hebrews 11 as witnesses in the race on earth-the billow of observers referenced in Hebrews 12:1: "Therefore, since we are surrounded by such a great cloud of witnesses...let us run with perseverance the race marked out for us."

"All through the Epistle (Hebrews), and particularly chapter 11," 'witnesses' perpetually signifies 'one who takes the stand., one who vouches for a specific certainty, and this is the more normal importance here. In later occasions it came to mean one who is devoted unto death in his witness bearing-a martyr. Nothing can be drawn from this passage with regards to the relation of the living and the dead."

So from an examination of the relevant Scriptures we conclude up two things: (1) Attempts by the living to speak with the dead are expressly "forbidden." (2) There is no scriptural support for the view that deceased holy people take an active, functioning, conscious part in the activities of the church militant.

"THIS IS FORBIDDEN"

◇◇◇◇◇

# Where Do I Go When I Die?

"Jesus answered him, 'I tell you the truth,
today you will be with me in paradise.'
(Luke 23:43).

"I desire to depart and be with Christ,
which is better by far."
(Philippians 1:23).

The inquiry is one that each thoughtful individual will ask at some time. Our sole resort for a definitive answer is the supernaturally enlivened disclosure in the Scriptures. It is normal for God's Word that each significant doctrine or truth is given broadened treatment some place in the hallowed volume.

For instance, Resurrection is examined finally in I Corinthians 15. In any case, there is no such stretched out treatment in reply to our inquiry above.

By the by, we are not left without clear suggestions of what lies ahead for the believer in the world to come.

Death includes the partition of the body and the spirit (utilizing the last term to signify the immaterial part of the individual). The body breaks down, however the soul lives on in cognizant and individual presence.

A few teachers hold the view that in the interim among death and the resurrection, the believer will be in an insubstantial state. Others are slanted to think, in view of II Corinthians 5:1-4, that the believer will be dressed with a "transitory body" until the resurrection, when the spiritual body will be received.

"Presently we realize that if the natural tent we live in is crushed, we have a working from God, an everlasting house in heaven, not worked by human hands. In the mean time we groan, yearning to be dressed with our heavenly abiding, in light of the fact that when we are dressed, we won't be discovered stripped (naked). For while we are in this tent, we groan and are loaded, in light of the fact that we don't wish to be unclothed yet to be dressed with our heavenly dwelling...(II Corinthians 5:1-4).

The general accord is by all accounts, we are in a cognizant presence, in spite of the fact that we are not yet in our spiritual bodies. We are not coasting around in space as imperceptible spirits, without the limit with respect to discourse or activity.

Nor are we sleeping or oblivious in an impermanent or dormant state. We are to be particularly alive and extremely near to Christ, for to be 'absent from the body' signifies 'to be present with the Lord."

There are numerous things about this subject we don't know and can't know for certain. Be that as it may, we do know with affirmation that at death the souls of believers go promptly to heaven, where they are totally and absolutely cheerful.

But then there is more and better to pursue. As somebody once put it, the minute we take the final breath on earth, we take our first breath in heaven. It was so with the dying thief, for did not our Lord say to him, "today you will be with me in heaven?"

After the thief voiced his request, "Jesus, remember

me when you come into your kingdom" (Luke 23:42), the Lord's answer did a lot to answer our inquiry.

We should not peruse excessively into the expressions of the thief, for he would have been exceptionally guiltless of religious philosophy. In any case, in them here is an early affirmation of His royalty.

The thief's dread of Christ's identity was without a doubt extremely restricted, yet the Holy Spirit had been working in his heart in reply to the Savior's supplication, and in his heart was the germ of faith that drew forward the Master's pregnant words.

It ought to be noticed that Jesus, as He some of the time does, did not answer the exact expressions of the man's appeal to but accomplished something endlessly more prominent. He conceded the craving of his heart. The criminal did not and couldn't realize that the correct expressions of his petition would not be satisfied for at least two thousand years, until the point that Christ enters completely into His Kingdom.

To the thief Jesus promised that to be absent from the body was to be quickly with the Lord. We may draw three deductions from His answer:

1. That the soul endures the breaking down of the body.
2. That spirit and body exist independently. While the body is still in the grave, the soul can be with Christ. The body of the thief would be discarded generally, however his soul would be in the quick nearness of Jesus Christ, in the place of departed spirits-heaven. His experience was not to be

oblivious rest, but rather cognizant association with Christ.

3. That there is no hole between the snapshot of death and the entry of the redeemed soul into the joy and happiness of time everlasting.

This raises another question: In the intermediate state, does the soul sleep?

It is battled by some religious gatherings that among death and the resurrection (a period for the most part named "the middle of the road express"), the soul "sleeps" - that is, exists in an oblivious express, a dreamless rest. This wonder is known as "soul sleep."

We know since Jesus said it on the cross, 'this day thou will be with me in heaven.'

The facts confirm that passing in Scripture is now and again alluded to as "sleep" (for instance, John 11:11; I Cor. 15:6, 18, 20, 51; I Thess. 4:13-15). Be that as it may, in these entries, sleep is basically a code word for death and isn't to be taken literally.

The setting makes that obvious. Jesus utilized the word in that sense when He told the discipless that Lazarus had "fallen asleep." They took His words actually, literally and reacted, "Master, in the event that he sleeps, he will show signs of improvement." Jesus let them know clearly, "Lazarus is dead" (John 11:11-14).

There is no entry in Scripture that insists that the soul sleeps. The individual rests, not the soul. The extraordinary issue that defenders of the "soul sleeps" hypothesis have never possessed the capacity to understand convincingly is the manner by which to translate a few entries of Scripture that instruct doubtlessly that there is close to home and cognizant presence among death and the resurrection. the story of Dives and Lazarus is one of these (Luke 16:19-31). How could the rich man be in cognizant torment in the event that he was sleeping?

It is questioned that Jesus did not give this story or episode to manage the cost of knowledge into a halfway state, but instead as a notice on the issues of life in our very own natural presence. While surrendering this might be valid, does it fundamentally debilitate all that He planned to instruct?

Furthermore, would he say he is in the meantime prone to misdirect us in the matter of the middle of the road state? He clearly proposed us to discover that the two Dives and Lazarus were alive and cognizant, or the anecdote would have no point by any means. The Bible says, "For me to live is Christ and to die is gain" (Phil. 1:21). How might it be gain to Paul if death brought only unconsciousness, or sleep?

# CHAPTER

# FOUR

◇◇◇◇◇

# Will Mansions Be Awaiting Us?

"In my Father's house are many mansions: if it were not so, I would have told you. I go to prepare a place for you. And if I go and prepare a place for you, I will come again, and receive you unto myself; that where I am, there ye may be also. (John 14:2-3).

"Trust me!" Our Lord encouraged his disciples. He spoke these words on the night prior to the cross to His truly cherished disciples, who were crushed at the possibility of His abandoning them. So He urged them to continue trusting in Him.

Nonetheless, the interpreter's utilization of "mansions" in the King James Version has given ascent in a few personalities to an idea the word was never proposed to pass on. Mansions, as utilized today, evokes the image of a superb natural chateau and has propelled numerous hymns.

Be that as it may, that was not all the importance of the word when Jesus utilized it. The word seems just rarely in Scripture, and in John 14:23 the first Greek is interpreted "dwelling place" the King James Version and "home" in the New International Version. It is an impartial word and comes no dream of magnificence, however just methods a "a dwelling place."

Understanding the genuine importance of the word more than makes up for any supposed loss, because Jesus added, "we will come to him and make our home with him" (v. 23). A home inhabited by the Trinity is no conventional place! Jesus assured us that the homes in heaven are changeless abodes, not temporary shacks, nor substandard lodging in heaven.

In this paragraph, the Lord was further assuring his disciples that the parting would be just impermanent. What's more, He promised a blissful, joyous reunion, saying as a result, "If I go, I will return. Try not to be cast down! He disclosed to them that in His Father's home there are "many rooms." No disciple need fear avoidance, there would be adequate space for all.

Another commonplace picture assures us that heaven will be no conventional place. Believers comprise the bride of Christ, and of them Jesus stated, "I never again call you servants...Instead, I have called you friends (John 15:15). This happy relationship ensures that we won't be housed in servants' quarters, but in a bridal suite.

The disciples were clearly confused with as to what His departure implied, so the Lord disclosed to them, essentially: "You trust in God? Trust also in me.

In our past relationship, have I at any point broken my word to you? In the event that my flight were not to your greatest advantage, would I not have let you know? Trust me!"

In a perfect world, home is a place where cherishing and providing for their children are all they need, where they train and order them affectionately and strongly, and where relatives appreciate uninhibited fellowship and fun-a position of love, understanding and security, where sorrows are together shared.

In any case, there are some who will scarcely make it home. Paul talks about one such: "he himself will be saved, however just as one escaping through the flames" (I Cor. 3:15). How much better to have an abundant entrance.

◇◇◇◇◇

## What Changes Will Be There?

"...the first paradise and the primary earth had passed away, and there was never again any ocean...

"I didn't see a sanctuary in the city...The city does not require the sun or the moon to sparkle on it..." (Revelation 21:1, 22,23).

It creates the impression that in paradise we will be free of much that we regard significant and irreplaceable at this point. For instance, there is no night there. Envision seven days without rest! What an aid night is the point at which we are bone tired. Yet, since the truth of paradise is far superior" than life on earth, there must favor in the apparently negative attributes incorporated into the book of Revelation.

Consider some of these beneficial absences.

1.  No Temple. "I didn't see a temple in the city" (21:22).

To a Jew, this would be as inconceivable as a city without a church would be to us. The excellent temple was the exceptional element and wonder of the natural Jerusalem. Its residents took great pride in it.

Matthew records, "Jesus left the temple and was leaving when his disciples came up to him to point out its structures" (24:1). The temple was to them the visible symbol of God dwelling in their midst, for God Himself had said to Moses, "Then have them make a sanctuary for me, and I will dwell among them" (Ex. 25:8).

In heaven, in any case, there is never again any requirement for a unique building set apart for the love of God, for God is Himself the temple. The earthly temple is supplanted by the prompt nearness of the omnipresent God. So we can say goodbye to troublesome building reserves and denominational contrasts and "love Him in spirit and truth!"

2.  No Sea. "...there was no longer any sea" (21:1).

A sealess heaven! This appears to be nearly as unthinkable as a world with no night. The sea fills such a colossal job in our life on earth that we can barely imagine its non-attendance (its absence). Be that as it may, there would be benefits.

Tempest and wreck would be a relic of past times. To the outcast or migrant, the sea implies detachment from home and friends and family, and the disjoining of valued kinships. As he wrote of his vision of heaven, John was himself encountering the forlornness of an outcast, an exile on the Patmos Isle.

The eager, persistent flood of the sea suitably symbolizes the vulnerability and unwelcome changes of life. So a sealess heaven would pass on to John's readers that there will be no more outcast or division, no more sundered friendships, no more depression, rather, the reunion or gathering with friends and family.

Rather than the sea there is a wonderful river flowing from the throne of God and of the Lamb down the extraordinary road of the city of God. On each side of the waterway there develops the tree of life, which yields its organic product consistently (22:2). Rather than the evils of the sea, heaven holds a nurturing, organic product (fruit-producing) river. The peruser will have no issue in translating the imagery (symbolism).

3.  No Death. "There will be no more death" (21:4). What a comfort, reassurance and consolation these six words pass on to the troubled heart. The king of dread and terror, the last enemy, will never have the capacity to rupture or breach the magnificent gates and disturb the bliss of heaven! No more passing bed vigils or funerals. The funeral wagon will have made its last voyage.

4.  No Mourning and Crying. "There will be no... mourning or crying" (21:4).

Grieving (Mourning) and crying caused by the occasion of deprivation or the assaults of wrongdoing will be no more. At some point or another the injury of mourning surpasses all of us on this earth.

In marriage, one accomplice should generally navigate that encounter, with its going with time of melancholy and misfortune.

The majority of us confront the loss of parents. Christians feel these things similarly as profoundly as others; we are not dehumanized by our feelings about what's to come. Be that as it may, we do have the advantage of the truth of the compensatory comfort of God and the hope for resurrection.

5. No Pain. "There will be no more...pain, for the old order of things has passed away." (21:4). No more joint inflammation. With the expansion of maturing one must face the squandering and crumbling of the body and the agony and shortcoming that regularly go with the procedure. For sure, at any phase of life we are at risk to encounter torment in changing degrees. All of this is absent in heaven.

6. No Hunger or Thirst. "Never again will they hunger; never again will they thirst" (7:16). Two of the most anguishing encounters individuals suffer will be exiled, banished. Consider what this will mean to keeping millions from Africa, India and different places on the earth who have overlooked what it resembles to have a full stomach! No one in heaven will ever feel the aches of appetite (hunger) of the misery of thirst.

7. No Tears. "He will wipe every tear from their eyes" (21:4). He will wipe away all tears from the essence of every native of heaven. All tears-those emerging from our very own transgression and disappointment, or from distress or loss, or those caused by others.

Since there will be not any more crying, there will be no more tears, or the event for them. On earth, tears will stream once more, but in heaven the Comforter will give lasting reassurance.

8. No Night. "There will be no night" (22:5). Following a long and tiring day, how welcome are the shades of night-one of God's choicest endowments. Our

tired bodies require whatever rest of night to recruit strength for the requests of the new day. Without a doubt the nonappearance of night would be an incredible disaster, not a gift. At that point for what reason is what is currently a mode of refreshment and recharging expelled from heaven?

There is a valid justification. Our changed bodies will never again need the recuperative procedure of rest. Valid and True, there will be abundant activity in heaven, but it will be without weariness or fatigue, for our bodies will be like His.

"Also, we excitedly anticipate a Savior from there, the Lord Jesus Christ, who...will transform our lowly bodies so that they will be like his glorious body" (Phil. 3:21).

There are numerous faculties in which night is helpful, yet Scriptures uncovers negative highlights also, for obscurity is representative of wrongdoing. "This is the verdict: Light has come into the world, but men loved darkness instead of light because their deeds were evil" (John 3:19).

Night is related with dull and abhorrent wrongdoings. Distress appears to be progressively strong amid the night, and torment increasingly intense. However, heaven presents another order. Rather than the dull night of tension and dread, there only the light beaming from the face of Jesus Christ (II Cor. 4:6).

9.  No Sun or Moon. "The city does not require the sun or moon to shine on it, for the glory of God gives it light, and the Lamb is its light" (21:23).

Heaven is washed in the eternal glory that proceeds from Him who depicted Himself as the Light of the World. There will be no requirement for outside, man-made lights. To all forever He is the light-bearer from whose face radiates the light of the glory of God. The gainful service of sun and moon is supplanted by the ceaseless brightening of the Son of Righteousness.

10. No Shut Gates. "On no day will its gates ever be shut" (21:25).

Since all that is abhorrent and unclean is prohibited and excluded from the heavenly city, (what a reality!), safety efforts will never again be required. There will be open access but perfect security. At that point Isaiah's prediction will be satisfied: "Your gates will always stand open, they will never be shut, day or night" (60:11).

# CHAPTER

# FIVE

◇◇◇◇◇

# What Is The Role Of Angels In Heaven?

"...when God brings his firstborn into the world. he says, 'Let all God's angels worship him.' In speaking about the angels he says, 'He makes his angels winds, his servants flames of fire." (Hebrews 1:6,7)

An Angel is characterized as an attendant, a delegate or messenger of God. The presence and ministry of holy messengers (angels) on earth and in heaven is referenced no less than three hundred times in the Bible, which is the only legitimate, authentic source of information about them.

Be that as it may, regardless of this successive notice, they get insignificant consideration (minimal attention) in the contemporary world, both secular and religious. This has made them be alluded to as the most overlooked or ignored personalities of Scripture.

Three frames of mind toward angels win among those to whom the Scriptures are not the final authority.

1. The presence of angels is recognized as an article of faith, however more remote than that, little interest is taken in their role.

2. Accounts of the activity of angels are taken as hyperboles, figures of speech passing on the possibility of glorious messages or of divine influence.

3. The subject is rejected carelessly as having no premise in fact - mere fantasy.

A comparable rationalistic frame of mind toward angels was experienced both by Jesus and by Paul, for "The Sadducees state that there is no resurrection, and that there are neither angels nor spirits" (Acts 23:8).

The Pharisees were not involved with this denial, but rather in our day the church at large appears to be nearly to have dropped the subject from thought and teaching. It was not always so in the church.

◇◇◇◇◇

## What Are Angels Like?

The standard origination of their appearance by numerous individuals is that they are envisioned as being in human frame with wings, wearing long, white robes.

In any case, from the Bible (the last expert) we discover that they are insignificant, profound creatures, despite the fact that now and again they accept human frame. They are spoken to as God's company, always at His administration. Seraphim and cherubim are depicted as winged (Isaiah 6:2), yet it isn't expressed that all holy messengers (angels) have wings, in spite of the fact that they may.

Since in appearance they are human-like, it has been simple for them to be confused with people. Now and again their brilliant and sparkling appearance has excited fear in the spectators.

Discussing a holy messenger, Matthew stated, "His appearance resembled lightning, and his clothes were white as snow. The guards were so afraid of him that they shook and became like dead men" (Matt. 28:33-4).

Angels give off an impression of being countless. Heaven

is overflowing with them. Jesus gave understanding into their numbers at the season of His capture in the Garden of Gethsemane; "Do you think I can't call on my Father, and he will at once put at my disposal more than twelve legions of angels?" (Matt. 26:53).

When it is remembered that a Roman legion could include anything from three thousand to six thousand men, the heavenly populace is hard to imagine. In Revelation 5:11 notice is made of the holy messengers (angels) circling the position of authority of God: "At that point I looked and heard the voice of numerous blessed messengers, numbering thousands upon thousands, and ten thousands times ten thousand."

Despite the fact that blessed messengers are radiant and heavenly identities, yet they are but created beings who have access to the presence of God (Ps. 103:20). They are of high intelligence, but our supernaturally settled connection to them comes as an astonishment.

To the Corinthian believers Paul asked a noteworthy inquiry: "Do you not know that we will judge angels?" (I Cor. 6:3). Jesus additionally uncovered that they "neither marry nor (are) given in marriage" (Matt. 22:30).

◇◇◇◇◇

# What Are The Angel's Activities?

1. On numerous critical occasions they ministered to the Lord-at His Birth, after the temptation in the desert, in Gethsemane, at the tomb of Joseph, and at the Ascension.

2. They have a special ministry "to believers" here on earth. "Are not all angels ministering spirits sent to serve those who will inherit salvation?" (Heb. 1:14). It would appear from this passage in heaven we will be amazed when we find how dynamically active heavenly attendants (angels) have been for our sake.

3. They have an special ministry to "children." "See that you don't look down on one of these little ones. For I reveal to you that their holy messengers in heaven always see the face of my Father in heaven" (Matt. 18:10).

4. They know about and rejoice over the salvation of the lost. "I tell you, there is rejoicing within the presence of the angels of God over one sinner who repents" (Luke 1'5:10).

5. At the Rapture, the holy messengers (angels) will be the gatherers (reapers). "The weeds are the children of the evil one, and the enemy who sows them is the devil. The harvest is the end of the age, and the harvesters are angels" (Matt. 13:38-39).

To outline:

* Angels worship and serve God.
* They minister to children and believers.
* They communicate God's messages to people.
* They execute judgment on God's enemies.
* They will be involved with the Second Advent.

# CHAPTER

# SIX

◇◇◇◇◇

# Rewards And Resurrection Bodies

Here is a searching word - the "motive" of our work is what matters. In that day God will test everything by His standard of truth, and if it meets with His endorsement, a reward will be given.

The reward isn't salvation, for salvation is of grace, altogether apart from works (Eph. 2:8-9). But this reward is for faithful service, because of salvation.

Who will get rewards?

"Blessed are you when men hate you, when they exclude you and insult you and reject your name as evil, because of the Son of Man. Rejoice in that day and leap for joy, because great is your reward in heaven." (Luke 6:22, 23).

The subject of rewards for the believer in heaven is one that is by all accounts thought of just sometimes by the conventional Christian, or even by the normal understudy of the Scriptures. It is without a moment's delay both a joyous and a solemn theme, and should fill in as a potent incentive for holiness of life.

There are spiritual dogmatists who respect the entire idea of rewards for service as a very second rate rate motivation. They compare it to offering sweet to a child that he will be good. Be that as it may, Jesus not the slightest way offered support to this perspective.

The verses at the head of this chapter show the reverse, as do numerous other of His statements. The Apostle Paul also teaches about rewards in several of his letters.

It barely need be said that no commendable

demonstrations of our own can win salvation, for that is a result of God's unmerited love. But, the simple truth that Jesus spoke of rewards for service on various occasions would indicate that He considered their granting an important article of faith.

In no way, not the slightest bit did He recommend or suggest that service was a method of accumulating merit and therefore receiving salvation. Eternal life is a gift, not a reward.

The dialect in which the concept of rewards is dressed is highly symbolic and allegorical and should be translated appropriately. Obviously, faithful service acquires rewards in this life and also in the life to come. Both are referenced to in the following verse:

"If I tell you the truth, Jesus said to them, no man who has left home or wife or brothers or parents or children for the sake of the kingdom of God will fail to receive many times as much in this age and, in the age to come, eternal life'" (Luke 18:29).

The New Testament opens with the Lord's promise of reward in the Beatitudes: "Blessed are you when people insult you, persecute you and falsely say all kinds of evil against you because of me. Rejoice and be glad, because great is your reward in heaven" (Matt. 5:11-12). This reward is for the person who endures slander and persecution for the sake of the Lord.

The New Testament closes with the Lord's assurance, "Behold, I am coming soon! My reward is with me, and I will give to everyone according to what he has done" (Rev. 22:12).

Since Jesus said that the reward for affliction borne

for His sake is great and is a cause for rejoicing, we should take His words seriously and not dismiss them cavalierly as some do.

Paul is equally definite on this point: "For we must all appear before the judgment seat of Christ, that each one may receive what is due him for the things done while in the body, whether good or bad" (II Cor. 5:10).

From this passage we discover that our past deeds will stand up to us at the judgment seat, however it is equally evident that there the salvation of the believer isn't at issue. That vital issue was settled perpetually at the Cross, when our substitute graciously bore the judgment that was justly because of us for our sins.

Because of that blessed occasion, Paul guaranteed adherents, "Through him (Christ), everyone who believes us justified from everything you could not be justified from by the law of Moses" (Acts 13:39). The blessed consequence is that "Therefore there is now no condemnation for those who are in Christ Jesus" (Rom. 8:1).

So the believer need treasure no dread of losing eternal life at the judgment seat. However, it may be protested, "Did not Paul have a fear of being a castaway?" When Paul wrote of that plausibility, it was not on the grounds that he was in fear of losing his salvation. "Castaway," as it is rendered in the King James Version of I Corinthians 9:27, is better rendered "disqualified."

Paul was speaking with regards to competing in the Isthmian games.

The fear he engaged was that, in the wake of having exhorted others how to run to win the coveted prize, he himself may be disqualified for the victor's crown. All things considered, everlasting life isn't a reward but a gift.

Every single genuine believer who stand before the judgment seat will qualify for heaven, however, not all will receive a similar reward. Somebody once stated, "Prizes will be determined more based on fidelity and suffering as opposed to on successful endeavors." We are, in any case, strongly exhorted to "watch out that you don't lose what you have worked for, but that you may be rewarded fully" (II John 8).

In the illustrations of the minas (Luke 19:11-27) and the talents (Matt. 25:14-30), Jesus taught that every believer has contrasting capacities and limits. That is something over which we have no control and for which we are not responsible. The parable of the minas teaches that where there is equal ability however unequal faithfulness, there will be a smaller reward.

Then again, the story of the gifts reveals to us that where there is unequal ability but equal faithfulness, the rewards will be the same. Christ's judgment and the reward bestowed will be according to the use we make of the open doors given to us.

These parables, and indeed the entire subject of rewards for service, underline the significance of how we act at this very moment. It is since we are deciding our future status and reward in heaven.

◇◇◇◇◇

# What Do The Promised Crowns Signify?

"Now there is in store for me the crown of righteousness..." (II Timothy 4:8).

The rewards promised in heaven are now and then spoken to by the image of a crown. In the Greek culture a crown may be either a headdress worn by a king or queen or a wreath worn as an image of victory.

Before considering the significance of the crown granted to victors, we ought to have an unmistakable origination of the idea of heaven's rewards, for we are adept to liken them with our natural reward framework-measure up to pay for equivalent work.

Merit is in this manner included. In any case, an eternal crown or heavenly crown doesn't involve compensation. In the heavenly reward, merit is explicitly excluded. Our Lord's word to His disciples makes this unmistakable and clear:

Heaven's rewards are each of the a matter of God's grace. They are God's generous recognition of self-less and sacrificial service.

The way that the worker who was enlisted to work just at the eleventh hour got indistinguishable wage from the person who had worked throughout the day underlies the way that a large portion of the wage he got was not earned, but rather was a liberal blessing from the master. When one of the full-time workers accused his lord of shamefulness, he answered, Companion, I am not being out of line to you. Didn't you consent to work for a denarius? Take your compensation and go. I need to give the man who was contracted last equivalent to I gave you. Don't I have the privilege to do what I need with my very own cash? Or on the other hand would you say you are jealous on the grounds that I am liberal? (Matt. 20:13-15)

We are not told definitely what frame the crowns in paradise will take, however John MacArthur see has a lot to recognize it: "Believers' reward aren't something you wear on your head like a crown...Your compensate in heaven will be your ability for service in heaven....Heaven's crowns are what we will experience, endless life, unceasing happiness, eternal service, and everlasting blessedness."

In the New Testament there are two Greek words deciphered "crown." One is diadema, an imperial turban worn by Persian kings. It is dependably the image of royal or royal poise. It alludes to the sort of crown Jesus gets. The other word is stephanos, the victor's crown, "image of triumph in the Olympic recreations or some challenge thus by metonmy, a reward or prize" (Vine, 2003). It was a crown of leaves or vines, wonderfully woven. This is the word that is utilized to mean the rewards of heaven.

Here are some of the crowns mentioned in Scripture.

1. Crown of Life.

"Blessed is the man who perseveres under trial, because when he has stood the test, he will receive the crown of life that God has promised to those who love him." (James 1:12)

"Be faithful, even to the point of death, and I will give you the crown of life." (Revelation 2:10)

This crown is bestowed in acknowledgment of continuing and triumphing over trial and persecution even to the point of suffering. The inspiration or motivation must be love for Christ.

## 2. Crown of Righteousness

"Now there is in store for me the crown of righteousness, which the Lord, the righteous Judge, will award to me on that day-and not only to me, but also to all who have longed for his appearing." (II Timothy 4:8)

## 3. Incorruptible Crown

"They do it to get a crown that will not last; but we do it to get a crown that will last forever." (I Corinthians 9:2)

This crown is won by the those who take a strive for mastery, for excellence. Here Paul is using the figure of the pentathlon with its colossal interest of physical stamina. The crown is granted to the disciplined.

## 4. Crown of Rejoicing

"For what is our hope, or joy, or crown of rejoicing? Are not even ye in the presence of our Lord Jesus Christ at his coming?" (I Thessalonians 2:19)

This is the crown of the soul-winner. It will be cause for rejoicing when, in heaven, we meet the those who have been won to Christ through our service (ministry). This crown is available to each believer.

## 5. Crown of Glory

"Be shepherds of God's flock that is under your care,

serving as overseers-not because you must, but because you are willing, as God wants you to be...And when the Chief Shepherd appears, you will receive the crown of glory that will never fade away." (I Peter 5:2-4)

This promised award for spiritual pioneers in the church ought to provide solid inspiration, motivation for sacrificial pastoral ministry.

Nonetheless, none of these crowns is granted automatically. There are qualifying conditions joined to each, and it is conceivable to foreit a crown through unwatchfulness. In the letter to the congregation at Philadelphia, the risen Lord cautioned the believers:

"I am coming soon. Hold on to what you have, so that no one will take your crown" (Rev. 3:11). This is a contemporary cautioning to us, also, who are regularly encompassed by competing claims for our love and loyalty.

◇◇◇◇◇

# What Will Our Resurrection Bodies Be Like?

"But someone may ask, 'How are the dead raised? With what kind of body will they come?' How foolish! What you sow does not come to life unless it dies. When you sow, you do not plant the body that will be, but just a seed....But God gives it a body as he has determined...." (I Corinthians 15:35-38)

Paul is hesitant about broadly expounding on the exact nature of the resurrection body of the believer, likely due to the lack of revealed actualities. However he makes a few extremely distinct explanations. About such subjects the philosopher and the scientist can make only educated estimates. With the Inspired Word in our grasp, be that as it may, we have certainty.

1.  It will be a spiritual body (I Cor. 15:44), however will be consummately adjusted to our heavenly environment.

2.  It will be a genuine body, not an apparition, but rather will be like that of the risen Christ, who challenged His followers, "Touch me and see."

3.  It will be a recognizable body, having personality with the physical body that has been laid to rest. After the resurrection Jesus discussed having "flesh and bones." The Apostles recognized Jesus.

To illuminate the issue, Paul at that point continues in I Corinthians 15 to draw correlations and complexities between the physical and the spiritual bodies.

4.  It will be an incorruptible body (v. 42). It will be deathless, not expose to decay.

5.  It will be a glorious body (v. 43), no more drawn out "The body of our humiliation," subject to the oppression of transgression and the assaults of Satan.

6.  It will be a powerful body (v. 43), having thrown off the feebleness, the frailty of its mortality.

While now the body is just a blemished vehicle of the spirit and regularly disappoints or frustrates it, in heaven the new body will be superbly, perfectly suited to conditions in its new sphere. "Also, similarly as we have borne the likeness of the earthly man, so will we bear the likeness of the man from heaven" (I Cor. 15:49).

It ought to be noticed that the expression "spiritual body" does not suggest that it is ethereal and spooky, but instead that it will be subject to the human spirit, not to our carnal wants, or our fleshly desires. What's more, the spiritual body will have the capacity to express preferable the believer's aspirations than can the earthly body.

There are two current misguided judgments about the spiritual body that require correction. (a) That it will be indistinguishable with the body that was buried. (b) That there is no natural (organic) association between the body that was buried and that which is raised. If these originations were so, there would be another creation, not a resurrection. We should recognize that there is mystery here, mystery that will be solved only in heaven.

In answering the question, "With what sort of body will they come?" Paul articulated four facts, which are shown in the development of a seed and in the assorted variety of creatures and of the sun, moon, and stars.

1.  What develops from seed we sow isn't by and large indistinguishable with what is sown (I Cor. 15:37). An acorn seed produces not an acorn seed but rather an oak, yet both appreciate a similar life drive.

2.  Every sort of seed has an unmistakable, God-given body (Gen. 1:11; I Cor. 15:38).

3.  The product of the seed sown has a organic connection with the seed from which it sprang. It's anything but a

new creation however is the result of something as of now in presence.

4. There is incredible decent variety in the bodies in the set of all animals, as in the heavenly kingdom (I Cor. 15:39-41).

If the resurrection body isn't organized identified with the body that is sown as it dies, there can be no resurrection. That we can't clarify this does not alter its truth. We should remember that there are other mysteries, maybe associated, that we have to live with.

Therapeutic (Medical personnel) individuals disclose to us that in a lifetime our aggregate body substance has been changed around multiple times, but then our own personalities have continued; we continue as before individuals. Our memory of past occasions stays healthy. This is a mystery, as well, yet it sheds some light on our problem.

In I Corinthians 15:42-44 Paul contrasts the old body from the new in four regards:

1. It is sown perishable but will be raised imperishable (v. 42).

There has been only a single body not subject to corruption (Ps. 16:10; Acts 2:27). At some point or another our physical bodies squander away. We as a whole are casualties of malady and, eventually, passing. In spite of the fact that the funeral car is presently pervasive, our spiritual bodies will be imperishable.

2. It is sown in dishonor but will be raised in glory (v. 43).

There is not anything beautiful or heavenly (glorious) about a rotting corpse. We discard it with deference in a grave or by incineration (cremation). Be that as it may, the resurrection body will be a glorious body, inconceivably more lovely and wonderful. This is assured on the grounds that "the Lord Jesus Christ, who, by the power that enables him to bring everything under his control, will transform our lowly bodies so they will be like his glorious body" (Phil. 3:20-21).

3. It is sown in weakness but will be raised in power (v. 43).

Unavoidably the "strength of youth yields to the frailty of age. A dead body is an image of shortcomings, weakness but our new body, like our Lord's will be described by power. Rest won't be important to mitigate exhaustion or recover spent vitality. Our abilities will be broadened and we will divert from the impediments of which we are so cognizant in life on earth.

4. It is sown a natural body; it will be raised a spiritual body (v. 44).

The natural body is adjusted to life in this world but isn't fitted for life in the following. "The spiritual body is the organ which is personally identified with the soul of man, similarly as his present body is personally identified with his earthly life." No longer will our bodies be liable to the laws that limit our physical life.

◇◇◇◇◇

# Our Lord's Resurrection Body Is The Pattern For Ours (Phil. 3:21, 22)

He ate with His disciples (John 21:9, 12, 13). He passed through closed doors (John 20:19). He showed up and vanished from sight. He professed to have flesh and bones (Luke 24:39). At the end of the day, there was a genuine connection and identity with His former body, minus a portion of the constraints (limitations) of that body.

The rendering, "our vile body: (Phil. 3:21) is one of the unhappier interpretations of the King James Version. "Our lowly body" is more progressively exact translation. Our bodies are presently subject to impediment and disintegration, they bind and cramp us, and they are bound to come back to their constituent components. Be that as it may, "we will be changed."

When our Lord returns, a wonderful, glorious transformation will be effected. Our lowly bodies will be like His glorious body, and will be bodies in which our longings and aspirations will find immaculate, perfect expression.

What Was Our Lord's Resurrection Body Like?

It was unquestionably not the same as that equivalent body before death.

1. There were three events when He was not perceived at first by His closet companions: "promptly toward the beginning of the day (early morning), Jesus remained on the shore, but the disciples did not realize that it was Jesus" (John 21:4).

At this, she turned and saw Jesus standing there, but she didn't realize that it was Jesus" (John 20:14). "Jesus himself came up and walked alongside them; however they were kept from recognizing him" (Luke 24:15,16).

2. While the Lord's resurrection body was in reality unique, it bore likenesses to His physical body. He said He had "flesh and bones" (Luke 24:39). He denied that He was a ghost (Luke 24:27, 39). He prepared breakfast for His men and ate with them (John 21:9-14; Luke 24:42,43).

3. Notwithstanding, He had the ability to go through closed doors (John 20:19). He was never again restricted by our limitations of time and space.

4. His was a genuine (real) body. In reply to Thomas's doubt, He broadened the welcome, "Put your finger here; see my hands" (John 20:27). Also, to Mary, "Don't hold on to me" (John 20:17).

Jesus gave fulfilling proof that He was only indistinguishable individual from before the Cross. He was recognized by His intimates who were currently prepared to die for Him-as the majority of them did.

It is interesting to take note of that our Lord's body retained its scars in the new body. Precisely what this connotes is hard to state. One intriguing proposal is that scars received as suffering over Christ's sake will endure here and there, not as imperfections but rather as eternal symbols or badges of honor.

# CHAPTER

# SEVEN

◇◇◇◇◇

# Heavenly Occupations

◇◇◇◇◇

## What Will We Do In Heaven?

"The throne of God and of the Lamb will be in the city, and his servants will serve him. They will see his face..." (Revelation 22:3,4)

The vast majority of what we are told about heaven, as we have seen previously, is framed in negative terms. A large portion of its unmistakable highlights lie in what isn't there, but we are not left without a depiction of positive highlights that make it famously desirable. A portion of these are as distinct articulations, similar to the passage at the head of this chapter. Others are in alluring metaphors and symbols. Paul's assurance that heaven is "better by far" than life here on earth promises us full satisfaction in the life beyond.

Here are some of the ways in which we will be occupied in heaven.

1.  "They will see his face, and his name will be on their foreheads" (Rev. 22:4).

This will be the pinnacle of heaven's joy and fulfillment. Christ will be the universal attraction. Up to this time, individuals have been venerating a God who is just partially visible.

In any case, we will have the unutterable joy of seeing Him face-to-face with nothing between us.

In our spiritual bodies we will have be able to do what was denied to Moses in his earthly body. When Moses asked the Lord, "Now show to your glory," the appropriate response he got was, "When my glory passes by, I will put you in a cleft in the rock and cover you with my hand until I have passed by.

Then I will remove my hand and you will see my back; but my face must not be seen" (Ex. 33:19, 22,23). In heaven, in any case, beholding the glory of God in the face of Jesus Christ will be a daily experience. We will walk each day "in the light of (His) presence" (Ps. 89:15).

Obviously, the unfallen blessed messengers can hold up under the "uncreated shaft," for Jesus said,"...their holy messengers in paradise dependably observe the essence of my Father in paradise" (Matt. 18:10). Afterward, we will impart to them that privilege.

Obviously, the unfallen angels can bear the "uncreated beam," for Jesus said,"... their angels in heaven always see the face of my Father in heaven" (Matt. 18:10). Afterward, we will share with them that privilege.

The noteworthiness of the expression in Revelation 22:4, "his name will be on their foreheads," is something we should, likewise, consider. The reference here is to the formal attire of the esteemed cleric (high priest): "They made the plate, the sacred diadem, out of unadulterated gold and engraved on it, similar to an engraving on a seal: Holy to the Lord. At that point they affixed a blue cord to it to attach it to the turban, as the Lord commanded Moses" (Ex. 39:30-31).

In Jewish speech an individual's name represents his or her character. So the plate on the turban of the devout priest marked him out as a blessed man, a holy man completely committed to God, and one who was to resemble Him in character. We need wait we get to heaven to have this distinctive mark.

2.   "...his servants will serve him" (Rev. 22:3).

What an honor to serve the King of Kings and Ruler of the universe! But ours will be service of a special kind. One author brings up that "the expressions of this content are noteworthy in that the Greek words for servant and serve are not identified with each other as they are in the English language.

The word servant implies truly 'a slave,' however the word serve is held in Scripture for one kind of service - the service of worship." That is the reason some modern advanced adaptations (versions) read, "His servants shall worship him." The Lamb of God on the throne will be the object of the adoring worship of the redeemed, who will render him, without hesitance, holy service.

3.   "And they will reign for ever and ever" (Rev. 22:5).

This implies, notwithstanding the benefit of rendering priestly service, we will have royal status-sharing with Christ His glory. Was it not that for which He prayed? "Father, I want those you have given me to be with me where I am, and to see my glory" (John 17:24).

There are three classes of people who in Scripture are said to share the glory of the enthroned Christ.

(a) The primary group consists of the individuals who had stayed faithful to Christ in the midst of the trials of this earthly life. Their service had not been flawless, but rather they had remained true despite opposition.

"You are the individuals who have remained by me in my trials. Also, I give on you a kingdom, similarly as my Father presented one me, so you may eat and drink at my table in my kingdom and sit on honored positions, making a decision about the twelve tribes of Israel" (Luke 22:28-30).

It ought to be noticed that in the Greek there is no article in the condition "I confer on you a kingdom." It is actually, "I appoint to you a kingdom," demonstrating royal rank and authority. As a recognition of their loyalty, they are accorded seats of honor at the heavenly dinner (banquet) we will without a doubt receive the same reward.

They will likewise "sit on thrones, judging the twelve tribes of Israel." In those days, as today, the king as supreme judge of the high court had lawful assessors who sat with him, and no doubt this was the figure the Lord had in mind.

(b) The second class of believers who reign with the Lord surely includes the martyrs for Christ, and may potentially incorporate all believers. "Do you not know that the saints will pass judgment on the world? And if you are to pass judgment on the world, are you not competent to judge trivial cases?" (I Cor. 6:2). "I saw thrones on which were situated the individuals who had been given authority to judge. And I saw the souls of the individuals who had been decapitated as a result of their testimony for Jesus and because of the word of God" (Rev. 20:4).

(c) The third group includes the individuals who are the overcomers among the churches. "To him who overcomes, I will give the right to sit with me on my throne, just as I overcame and sat down with my Father on his throne" (Rev. 3:21). "To him who overcomes and does my will to the end, I will give authority over the nations..." (Rev. 2:26).

Overcoming includes strife, hardship and battle, and this promise is to the those who have been faithful and have persevered in battling the battles of the Lord. Paul had this at the top of the priority list when he spoke about the crown laid up for him since he could say with truth, "I have finished the race, I have finished the race, I have kept the faith" (II Tim. 4:7,8).

We should remember, anyway that while we reign with Christ in glory, we will still be His servants. Or better still to follow the example of Him who, while still on earth, stated, "I am among you as one who serves" (Luke 22:27).

4.    Heaven will be a worshiping community.

The most elevated activity in heaven will be to ascribe to the triune God our unconstrained and unrestricted worship and love. The accompanying passage is representative, in capsule form, of the worship that will be offered.

At whatever point the living creatures give glory, honor and thanks to him who sits on the throne and who lives for ever and ever, the twenty-four older elders fall down before him who sits on the throne and worship him who lives for ever and ever. They lay their crowns before the throne and say: "You are worthy, our Lord and God, to receive glory and honor and power, for you created all things, and by your will they were created and have their being." (Revelation 4:9-11)

# CHAPTER

# EIGHT

◇◇◇◇◇

# What Place Will Music Have?

"They held harps given them by God and sang the song of Moses the servant of God and the song of the Lamb..." (Revelation 15:2,3)

Music will in fact have a prominent place in the common existence (life) of heaven, even as it did in Israel's tabernacle and temple. There were no less than 288 performers occupied with the services of Solomon's temple (I Chron. 25:1,7).

Vocal, choral, and instrumental music add to the worship of the congregation. Among the instruments referenced regarding the temple (sanctuary) service are cymbals, psalteries, harps, trumpets, cornets, funnels, and other unspecified stringed instruments. A symphony is no advanced expansion to the worship of the sanctuary! The twenty-four elders are portrayed as every one having a harp, obviously going with themselves as they sing the praises of God (Rev. 5:8,9).

The apostle John had a preview of heaven's great music and attempted to pass on the impression it made on him: "And I heard a sound from paradise like the thunder of rushing waters and like a boisterous ring of thunder. The sound I heard resembled that of harpists playing their harps. Furthermore, they sang another melody before the throne" (Rev. 14:2,3).

It was another song, since heaven's melodies never become worn out. We before long feel sick of oft-rehashed chorales. We will in general go into unbiased when singing psalms we have sung from your childhood. In any case, heaven's music and melody is in every case crisp and new. No dissonant note will ever bump on the ear in heaven.

From the looks of heaven given in the book of Revelation, no doubt, in the event that one were not singing, one would feel somewhat out of it, for singing is plainly the "in" work out (exercise). All through the book of Revelation, diverse gatherings at fitting minutes get their own music commitment in praise to God.

The way that they were singing "another song" may demonstrate that heaven's music will be not quite the same as earth's, in spite of the fact that God is the creator of both. We as a whole have our inclinations and aversions in music, however we can make sure that the music of heaven will be so sweet, so agreeable, so stylishly satisfying and inspiring that nobody's taste will be offended. We can foresee some charming, pleasant surprises in the musical realm.

# CHAPTER

# NINE

◇◇◇◇◇

# The Second Advent And Judgment

◇◇◇◇◇

## What Will The Second Advent And The Judgment Mean To Us?

"Try not to be flabbergasted at this, for a period is coming when all who are in their graves will hear his (the Son of Man's) voice and turn out-the individuals who have done good will rise to live, and those who have done evil will rise to be condemned." (John 5:28,29)

It is neither conceivable nor important to incorporate a correct timetable for these wonderful occasions; it is the total conviction of them that is vital." man is bound to bite the dust once, and after that to confront judgment." (Heb. 9:27). We should remember that when these occasions do occur, the proportions of reality as we presently know them will have no pertinence.

However, talking in wording with which we are well-known, would it not be sensible to presume that, since the "day of salvation" has reached out more than two centuries, we require not endeavor to pack the Day of judgment into a concise period?

On the other hand, does this judgment essentially require quite a while as we probably are aware it? In nowadays of the wonders of the Web, the PC world and TV and the limitlessly more prominent wonder of the human mind, combined with the omniscience of God, the gradualness of our legal procedures manages no correlation.

It is an entrenched marvel that, in emergency, the entire substance of an actual life might be flashed before the mind of an individual in a snapshot of time.

In this book we are concerned just with the judgment of believers at the bema. This is a standout amongst the most critical occasions associated with the arrival of Christ, so far as the believer is concerned.

"For we must all show up before the judgment seat of Christ, that every one may get what is expected him for the things done while in the body, regardless of whether good or bad" (II Cor. 5:10).

Does this imply we should wait until the point that that day to know whether we are saved or lost? Does Scripture not instruct that after believing in Jesus Christ we go from death to life and won't come into condemnation?

In reality it does. The explanation of II Corinthians 5:10 lies in the way that Scripture perceives two sorts of judgment.

There is the judgment in criminal procedures where the judge sits on the seat, hears the proof, and chooses the blame, judgment, or vindication of the individual charged.

At that point there is the judgment of the umpire, or arbitrator who, as at the Olympic amusements, rises his judgment seat to articulate the champ and grant the prize, in light of the fact that the victor has run decently, fairly and well. Obviously, the conclusion is that the individuals who have not run fairly and well "suffer loss" and win no prize. It is this second judgment situate that Paul has in view in this verse.

An individual's interminable predetermination is as of now decided in this life, as indicated by regardless of whether the person has trusted in Christ for salvation. "So at that point, every one of us will give a record of himself to God" (Rom. 14:12). Hardly any verses of Scripture are more soul-looking than this.

The judgment seat of Christ, at that point, is His "umpire" situate. The basic role of His judgment is to survey and reward believers for the way in which they have utilized their chances and released their responsibilities. The premise on which we will be judged is expressed in clear terms: "that every one may get what is expected him for the things done while in the body, regardless of whether good or bad."

However, motives as well as deeds will be considered. "Along these lines judge nothing before the delegated time; wait till the Lord comes. He will bring to light what is hidden in darkness and will expose the motives of men's hearts" (I Cor. 4:5).

In a very penetrating paragraph Paul tells us how this process is carried out:

"For other foundation can no man lay than that is laid, which is Jesus Christ. Now if any man build upon this foundation gold, silver, precious stones, wood, hay, stubble: Every man's work shall be made manifest: for the day shall declare it, because it shall be revealed by fire, and the fire shall try every man's work of what sort it is. If any man's work abide which he hath built thereupon, he shall receive a reward. If any man's work shall be buried, he shall suffer loss: but he himself shall be saved; yet so as by fire." (I Corinthians 3:11-15)

What do gold, silver, and expensive stones symbolize? It is well to look at this subject in perspective of the genuine conceivable outcomes certain in the passage. What will be considered in the assessment?

1. Our Testimony to Christ – Philippians 2:16.
2. Our Suffering for Christ – I Peter 4:13.
3. Our Faithfulness to Christ – Luke 12:42,43.
4. Our Service for Christ – I Corinthians 3:8.
5. Our Generosity to Christ – II Corinthians 9:6; I Timothy 6:17-19.
6. Our Use of Time for Christ – Ephesians 5:15,16; Colossians 4:5.
7. Our Exercise of Spiritual Gifts – Matthew 25:14-28; I Peter 4:10.
8. Our Self-Discipline for Christ – I Corinthians 9:24,25.
9. Our Winning of Souls for Christ – I Thessalonians 2:19.

The bema isn't all joy and the triumphant of prizes for all believers. Paul told the Corinthian Christians that, similarly as the stars vary in glory, so also will the holy people (I Cor. 15:41,42).

Some will be embarrassed when He comes in view of unfaithfulness to Him, of persistence in known sin, or of having been ashamed of Him before people," And now, dear children, continue in him, so that when he appears we may be confident and unashamed before him at his coming" (I John 2:28).

Some will suffer loss because they have utilized wood,

hay, and straw in building on the foundation, and these materials can't withstand fire.

"If (any man's work) is burned up, he will suffer loss; he himself will be saved, but only as one escaping through the flames" (I Cor. 3:15).

Will we be among the individuals who get the full reward and have an abundant passageway into Christ's kingdom, or will we be among the individuals who are embarrassed, ashamed and suffer loss?

◇◇◇◇◇

# What Will The Second Advent Mean To Christ?

"Father, I want those you have given me to be with me where I am, and to see my glory, the glory you have given me because you loved me before the creation of the world." (John 17:24).

The natural narrow-mindedness of even the regenerate human heart is uncovered by our tendency to think about the Lord's arrival more regarding what it will mean to us-how the going with occasions will influence us-than of what it will mean to Him.

We are appropriately excited at the prospect of our eminent legacy in Christ, yet would we say we are similarly excited at the possibility of His inheritance in us? Here is Paul's supplication: "I ask also that the eyes of your heart might be enlightened in order that you may know the hope to which he has called you, the riches of his glorious inheritance in the saints,and his incomparably great power for us who believe" (Eph. 1:18,19).

What thought we have given to His glorious inheritance in us? Do we give careful consideration to His enthusiastic desire and expectation of His wedding day? Is His crowning liturgy day prominent in our minds?

Think about the startling complexity between His first approach and His second. At that point He came in poverty and humiliation; soon He will accompany unimaginable wealth and riches. At that point He came in weakness; soon He will come in incredible power. The He came in loneliness; soon He will come joined by His hosts of angels and the company of the redeemed.

He came as a man of sorrows, distresses; soon He will accompany brilliant and unalloyed happiness. At that point in joke men put a reed in His hand; soon He will employ the staff of all universal dominion. Men squeezed a crown of acanthus thistles upon His temples; soon He will come adorned with the numerous diadems He has won.

He was blasphemed, reviled, denied, deceived, betrayed; soon every knee will bow to Him, recognizing Him as King of Kings and Lord of Lords.

In His supplication to his Father, He made only a single individual request: "I need those you have given me to be with me where I am, and to see my glory" (John 17:24).

This petition uncovers the profound longing of His heart. These falling flat men meant a lot to Him-thus do we. When He comes back again, this longing will have its fulfillment so we will be for ever with the Lord." But in the light of His greatness and majesty and holiness, do we not cry out with the psalmist in amazed wonder,"...what is man that you are mindful of him, the son of man that you care for him?" (Ps. 8:4).

When He comes back again, He will be fully satisfied with the result of His so expensive sacrifice; "He shall see of the travail of his soul, and will be satisfied" (Isa. 53:11). He will then encounter the consummation of "the joy set before him."

This is a part of the joy set before Him.

Christ's return will result in His unceasing association with His bride, the church, which He purchased with His own blood. For Him, with respect to us, that will mean the happy joy of the wedding dinner of the Lamb and endless communion and fellowship.

When He returns, it will be to receive the kingdom of which He spoke such so much on earth. When He first came to His very own people and offered Himself as their king, their reaction was, "we won't have this man to rule over us." But finally His Kingship will be all around recognized and confessed.

◇◇◇◇◇

## What Will The Second Advent Mean To Satan?

"Now have come the salvation and the power and the kingdom of our God, and the authority of his Christ. For the accuser of our brothers, who accuses them before God day and night, has been hurled down." (Revelation 12:10)

For nobody will the return of Christ have more prominent and more extensive criticalness than for Satan, the detestable sovereign of this world. Scripture presents a steady picture of two adversary kingdoms going up against one another on the world scene-the kingdom of Satan and his flunkies, his minions are aligned with evil individuals in their arrangement to crush the kingdom of God and impact the ruin and demolish of mankind.

At the end of the age, Satan is found in collusion with the beast and the false prophet. These three, joined in a typical reason to vanquish Christ and secure control of the entire world, frame a vile trinity of fiendishness. While on earth, Jesus perpetrated a staggering annihilation on Satan-first in the allurement in the desert, however overwhelmingly in the Cross.

Christ "partook in (our) humankind so that by his death he may destroy him who holds the power of death-that is, the devil and free the individuals who for their entire lives were held in subjection by their fear of death" (Heb 2:14,15).

It was for this very purpose Christ came to earth the first time: "He who does what is sinful is of the devil, on the grounds that the devil has been sinning from the beginning. The reason the Son of God appeared up was to destroy the devil's work" (I John 3:8).

At Calvary that triumph was accomplished gloriously, and the sentence of doom was passed.

The blessed result was that, "having disarmed the powers and authorities, he made an open exhibition of them, triumphing over them by the cross" (Col. 2:15).

As far back as Calvary, the vaunted power of the enemy has been broken. His capacity isn't inherent, it is derived. He isn't invincible but vulnerable. He isn't triumphant yet damned. He and his associates are reserved for a last and future judgment, which is described in Revelation 20:7-10:

When the thousand years are over, Satan will be discharged from his jail and will go out to deceive the countries in the four corners of the earth-God and

Magog-to accumulate them for battle...They marched over the breadeth of the earth and encompassed the camp of God's people, the city he loves. But fire descended from heaven and ate up them.

And the devil, who deceived them, was thrown into the lake of burning sulfur, where the beast and the false prophet had been thrown. They will be tormented day and night for ever and ever.

So one of the blessed absences from heaven will be Satan the tempter, the accuser, the deceiver. There will be no more temptations coordinated at the feeble spots of our temperament. No more raking up of old sins and unwarranted allegations or accusations. No more double dealings play on our ignorance and credulity. Nothing unclean or defiling will ever enter heaven through those magnificent pearly gates. Glory be! Hallelujah! Hallelujah!

# CHAPTER

# TEN

◇◇◇◇◇

# New Heavens And New Jerusalem

◇◇◇◇◇

## The New Heavens And The New Earth

"But in keeping with his promise, we are looking forward to a new heaven and a new earth, the home of righteousness." (II Peter 3:13)

"Then I saw a new heaven and a new earth, for the first heaven and the first earth had passed away, and there was no longer any sea." (Revelation 21:1)

In this final series of visions conceded to John, we have gone to the peak of the purposes for God and to scenes that outperform the most astounding desire for the holy people. We are transported from time to time everlasting. Chapters 21 and 22 of Revelation are the most spectacular and sensational of the entire book and depict a stunning picture of what heaven will be like.

Chapter 20 closes with the words, "he was thrown into the lake of fire" (v. 15). Be that as it may, in the accompanying two chapters, in striking difference, we are given the glories and splendor of the heaven in which the redeemed will spend time eternity.

The Hebrews had long valued and cherished the dream of new heavens and a new earth where sin, sorrow, and suffering would be no more. The prophet Isaiah verbalized that longing: "Behold, I create new heavens and a new earth. The former things will not be remembered, nor will they come to mind" (Isa. 65:17).

John saw the new heavens and the new earth. He saw them in a vision, but knew that they would come into reality in a day yet future. He saw a super-world, the home of righteousness, which God had promised through the prophets (Acts 3:21).

In flaming metaphor Peter portends the technique by which this colossal transformation, this metamorphosis and renovation will occur.

"But the day of the Lord will come like a thief. The heavens will disappear with a roar; the elements will be destroyed by fire, and the earth and everything in it will be laid bare...That day will bring about the destruction of the heavens by fire, and the elements will melt in the heat. But in keeping with his promise we are looking forward to a new heaven and a new earth, the home of righteousness." (II Peter 3:10-13)

The old physical earth that has been the focal point of so much sin, revolt, and slaughter has vanished in this vision, as have the heavens (not the paradise where God's throne is). Those heavens have been where Satan has carried on his activities. Since he contaminates all that he touches, they should be cleansed by flame.

Since this world has also been the theater in which the drama of redemption has been enacted, it will, phoenix-like, rise from its fiery debris by the power of God, to another and inconceivable glory. The old Jerusalem had been stained with the blood of prophets and saints, and, most despicably of all, with the blood of God's Son. Be that as it may, no more blood will flow, and the New Jerusalem will be the home of the righteous.

It is intriguing that the only qualifying statement in

this passage about the new heavens and earth is that "there was never again any sea" (Rev. 21:1). The sea is an symbol of agitation, unrest and shakiness. Prior on in John's vision, it was from the sea that the satanic beast arose.

"Also, I saw a beast leaving the sea. He had ten horns and seven heads, with ten crowns on his horns, and on each head a blasphemous name" (Rev. 13:1). "Then the angel said to me, "The waters you saw, where the whore sits, are people groups, multitudes, nations and languages" (Rev. 17:15).

The surging sea speaks to the nations of the world in their perpetual clash, conflict with each other. But in the rejuvenated heavens and earth all will be peace and serenity.

The picture is of a universe transformed, culminated, cleansed of everything that is detestable and evil and that exalts itself against God. It is "new," not in the feeling of being a new creation, but of being new in character-a commendable milieu for the residence of God and His redeemed people. It is new a because of the presence of a new community of people, absolutely faithful to and loyal to God and to the Lamb.

We can't tell what the new creation will be like, for no details are given. The way that there will be no more sea could be an indication that the entire order of nature will be changed.

◇◇◇◇◇

# The New Jerusalem

"I saw the Holy City, the new Jerusalem, coming down out of heaven from God, prepared as a bride beautifully dressed for her husband." (Revelation 21:2)

This well known portrayal, the equivalent of which can't be found in some other writing of the ancient world, is the manner in which one author terms the vision of the New Jerusalem recorded in Revelation 21.

The new heavens and new earth must have a new metropolis with regards to their dignity and splendor. Also, God will send it down from heaven - the Holy City, the New Jerusalem.

In this depiction of an literal city of gold and pearl and precious stones, or should John's vision be translated symbolically? Distinctive researchers hold disparate perspectives for which they can progress conceivable contentions.

A strong case for the representative elucidation is made by G. H. Lang in his "Revelation of Jesus Christ;" I quote it finally in light of the fact that it appears to accord more with the entire tenor of the book of Revelation than the contradicting view. Lang feels that an exacting translation is unsatisfactory in view of characteristic challenges. I will in general concur.

A City can be so shaped, is to me in any event, so incomprehensible as to choose that this part isn't a portrayal of anything concrete. John is worried about spiritual states, not material substances.

In any case, these images and figures do have

wonderful reality behind them. The drop of the city, albeit communicated as far as a vision, has profound spiritual essentialness and is planned to pass on to our natural personalities the unbelievable glory that awaits us in heaven.

◇◇◇◇◇

## What Does The City Represent?

John will tell us himself:

One of the seven angels who had the seven bowls full of the seven last plagues came and said to me, "Come, I will show you the bride, the wife of the Lamb." And he carried me away in the Spirit to a mountain great and high, and showed me the Holy City, Jerusalem, coming down out of heaven from God. It shone with the glory of God…"

(Revelation 21:9-11)

It ought to be noted that the angel did not undertake to clarify the imagery, but rather just demonstrated to him the bride. The city was the bride!!

There is a parallel to this in chapter 5:5,6:

Then one of the elders said to me, "Don't weep! See, the Lion of the tribe of Judah…has triumphed. He is able to open the scroll and its seven seals."

Then I saw a Lamb, looking as though it had been slain, standing in the center of the throne….

The bride - a city. The lion - a Lamb.

I would present that it is sensible to derive to the city is an image of the perfect church as God imagined it first and conceived it in the beginning, and as it will be in the end- "without stain or wrinkle or some other blemish"

(Eph. 5:27). The church as it is on earth presently is just a poor shadow of the transcendent wonder of the church as it will be in the future.

In Revelation 21:1-4, 22-23, John identifies a few highlights of life on earth that will never again be present in the Holy City-no more sea, tears, death, grieving, pain, no sanctuary, no need of the light of sun or moon. As these absences from heaven have just been discussed, no further remark is vital here, but to state that we completely reverse the sadness, bitterness and miseries of earth, we can gain some thought of the joys and bliss of heaven.

The focal and most imperative element of the New Jerusalem is reported from the throne; "And I heard an uproarious voice from the throne saying, 'Now the dwelling of God is with men, and he will live with them. They will be his people, and God himself will be with them and be their God" (Rev. 21:3,4).

Israel had known something of God's presence in its midst in the images of the ark of the covenant and in the pillar of cloud and fire, but it had relinquished that benefit through its repeated failure and apostasy. Now the promise made to the Hebrews in their desert venture discovers full and glorious fulfillment: "I will look on you with favor...I will put my dwelling among you, and I will not abhor you. I will walk among you and be your God, and you will be my people" (Lev. 26:9-12).

In summary, the city of God and the new heavens and new earth are the peak of the whole plan of redemption. God isn't content with just fixing the attacks that transgression (sin) and Satan have fashioned in the excellent world He made.

He creates a new world, the home of that far outperforms the one demolished by Satan. He could have reproduced the first Eden, but that would have held the likelihood of a reiteration of the Fall, with all its unfortunate outcomes.

His arrangement is better by far. He sets up a new world and a new world order based on the redemptive work of the Lamb of God, along these lines promising that there will be no repeat of the shades of malice that have tormented humankind. With Satan at long last and always bound and with nothing that defiles ready to enter our heavenly home, we will indeed prove that to be with Jesus Christ in heaven is much better.

◇◇◇◇◇

## The Lamb's Book Of Life

What does it mean to have one's name written in the Lamb's Book of Life?

The illustration of books of record happens all through Scripture, starting with Moses' request to God to be "blotted out" of God's book as a atonement for the wrongdoings (sins) of the general population of Israel (Ex. 32:32). This figure is drawn from the registers of the tribes of Israel. Its last appearance is in the content we are considering.

Concerning the judgment before the Great White Throne, we read, "Then I saw a great white throne...And I saw the dead, great and small, standing before the throne, and books were opened. Another book was opened, which is the book of life. The dead were judged according to what they had done as recorded in the books" (Rev. 20:11,12).

One set of books, then, contains the record of every

individual's life-history. The other book is the Lamb's Book of Life. The primary record can bring judgment, for all have missed the mark regarding God's benchmarks (Glory). In the Book of life are recorded the names of the individuals who have atoned of their transgressions (sins) and practiced saving faith in Jesus Christ as Redeemer and Savior.

"Keep in mind that it relies upon ourselves whether our names are written there or not. It is available to anybody to do only that. A living faith in Christ, the Lamb of God who "removes the sin of the world," is the sole condition for having our names written in that book, and that establishes our international ID through the pearly gates.

Why not make sure beyond a shadow of a doubt of heaven by opening your heart to Jesus Christ the Savior and Lord at this moment, welcoming Him to enter, to cleanse it from wrongdoing (sin), and to make it His permanent dwelling place? Jesus Christ gives affirmation, "In the event that anybody hears my voice and opens the door, I will come in and eat with him, and he with me" (Rev. 3:20).

Best Of All – Jesus Is With Us!

# CHAPTER

# ELEVEN

◇◇◇◇◇

# Heaven In The Bible: (The Old Testament)

◇◇◇◇◇

## Enoch

The Bible's longest-lived man was the acclaimed Methuselah (969 years of age), however Methuselah's grandfather, Jared, was close (962 years of age). Be that as it may, breaking the pattern was Jared's son, and Methuselah's father, Enoch. "So all the times of Enoch were three hundred and sixty five years.

What's more, Enoch walked with God; and "he was not," for God took him" (Gen. 5:23,24). This expression "he was not" has prompted much theory. Is it true that he was taken into heaven? Since Enoch "walked with God," we should accept he was a good man, so heaven would have been a proper reward. Jews and Christians have generally trusted that he was "translated" into heaven, similarly as, hundreds of years after the fact, the great prophet Elijah was taken into heaven without experiencing death.

◇◇◇◇◇

## Eternal Life In The Book Of Daniel

The Israelites had no reasonable origination of an existence in the wake of death. The one special case to this is the book of Daniel, one of the last Old Testament books to be composed. "Furthermore, a considerable lot of the individuals who rest in the dust of the earth shall awake, some to everlasting life, some to shame and everlasting contempt. The individuals who are astute will sparkle like the brilliance of the firmament, and the individuals who turn many to righteousness like the stars everlastingly. These words from Daniel 12:2,3 are the only unequivocal mention in the Old Testament of a heaven and a hell.

◇◇◇◇◇

## Elijah Into Heaven

The extraordinary prophet Elijah had a few encounters with devilish Queen Jezebel's likewise fiendish spouse, King Ahab. He anticipated fate for both Jezebel and Ahab, predictions that worked out as expected. Elijah's successor, Elisha, saw his master taken to heaven in a fiery chariot (II Kings 2).

Elijah turned into an symbol of Israel's prophets, and since he did not die and was taken to heaven, individuals started to trust that he would some time or another arrival to turn the people back to God. The prophet Malachi anticipated that God would send Elijah before the "day of the Lord" to set up the people. Jesus said that John the Baptist in reality was (spiritually speaking) Elijah returned (Matt. 11:14).

◇◇◇◇◇

# Job And The Afterlife

The book of Job is an ageless look at the suffering of a saintly man. Run of the mill of the Old Testament, the book appears to expect that any good that a man has is in this life only, not in the great beyond. At a certain point in the book, Job mourns that "man dies and is laid away; to be sure, he breathes his last and where is he?"

At that point he brings up the agonizing issue: "If a man dies, will he live again?" (Job 14:10, 14). Later in he book he makes a stirring insistence: "I know that my Redeemer lives, and He will stand at last on the earth; and after my skin is destroyed, this I know, that in my flesh I shall see God" (Job 19:25,26).

Brought up in a culture that did not have an unequivocal belief in heaven, was Job envisioning one? Maybe. Surely has phrase "I know that my Redeemer lives" go into the Christian vocabulary, being connected to Christ.

◇◇◇◇◇

# A Whisper Of Immortality

Psalm 16 is cited in the New Testament as applying to Jesus' death and resurrection. Think about how the hymn closes: "You won't leave my spirit in Sheol, nor will You enable Your Holy One to see corruption. You will show me the path of life" (v. 10,11).

While the Old Testament for the most part sees Sheol as the inauspicious last resting spot of everybody, there are insights, for example, this psalm that God won't leave all righteous people there-that something better is in store. The early Christians connected the psalm to Jesus, whom God did not leave in Sheol (the grave, that is), nor did He enable Him to decay. (See Acts 2:27; 13:35).

◇◇◇◇◇

# The House Of The Lord Forever

Psalm 23, which starts, "The LORD is my shepherd," is a standout amongst the most commonplace Bible entries. The "Shepherd Psalm" is a contacting melody of acclaim for God's assurance and care. Note the completion: "Without a doubt goodness and mercy shall follow me all the days of my life; and I will dwell in the house of the LORD forever.."

Is this a confirmation of heaven? Most likely not, since the Psalm don't generally express any faith in a heaven. The "house of the LORD" is presumably the sanctuary in Jerusalem. Be that as it may, Christians have adored this song as much as the Jews did, and its last verse has been taken to allude to eternal bliss with the Lord.

◇◇◇◇◇

# Swords Into Plowshares

The expression, utilized by the prophets Isaiah and Micah, alludes to moving from a condition of war to a province of God-sent peace. "They will beat their swords into plowshares, and their lances into pruning hooks; nation will not lift up sword against nation, neither will they learn war any more" (Isa. 2:4; Mic. 4:3).

Human instinct being what it is, Christians appeal to God for (but don't really expect) the sort of peace to happen in our world. For such a great condition of things we need to wait for heaven.

◇◇◇◇◇

# And A Little Child Shall Lead Them

Isaiah the prophet imagined a period and place (obviously heaven, not earth) in which the childishness and fierceness of this present life will be no more: "The wolf likewise will abide with the lamb, the leopard will rests with the youthful goat, the calf and the youthful lion and the fatling together; and a little child will lead them...

The nursing child will play by the cobra's opening, and the weaned child will put his hand in the viper's den. They will not hurt nor decimate in all My holy mountain" (Isa. 11:6-9). Sounds lovely, isn't that right? These words have propelled various craftsmanships, and have been cited or implied on many occasions.

◇◇◇◇◇

# The Lord Is There

A large portion of Ezekiel's prophecies concern the reestablishing of the country of Israel, but many readers interpret the prophecies as applying to the end of time. Think about the end of the book: Ezekiel has been portraying another Israel, however his words appear to apply to a heavenly habitation.

Ezekiel's prophecy closes, "and the name of the city from that day will be: "THE LORD IS THERE" (48:35). How close this is to Revelation: "Behold, the tabernacle of God is with men, and He will dwell with them, and they will be His people. God Himself will be with them" (Rev. 21:3).

# CHAPTER

# TWELVE

◇◇◇◇◇

# What Jesus Taught

◇◇◇◇◇

## Heaven And Hell: A New View

The Old Testament says next to no regarding life following death (afterlife). For the general population of Israel, the principle objective in life was to live on earth and have a good relationship with God and with other individuals. After death...what? The majority of the Israelites did not conjecture about that. They concentrated on this life.

In any case, the New Testament clarifies that God designed people for the afterlife -a happy, joyous afterlife, with Him (heaven) or a despondent, unhappy, hopeless life following death separated from Him (hell). Jesus said a great deal regarding God's love and kindness, but also a ton about the end result for us when we reject that love. By our very own decision we can turn to God. Or then again we can live for ourselves, disregarding God and ignoring our duties to other people.

◇◇◇◇◇

## The Kingdom Of God

The "Kingdom of God" and the "Kingdom of Heaven" are referenced ordinarily in the New Testament, more often than not by Jesus. Mark 1:15 starts the narrative of Jesus along these lines: "The time is fulfilled, and the Kingdom of God is at hand. Repent, and trust in the gospel."

In any case, Jesus clarified that the Kingdom isn't a place or a political substance. He told Pilate, "My Kingdom is not of this world" (John 18:36). "Kingdom of God," as Jesus utilized it, signified "rule of God-the condition of God's will winning in men's lives. As Jesus put it, "The Kingdom of God is inside you" (Luke 17:21).

◇◇◇◇◇

## Theirs Is The Kingdom Of Heaven

"Blessed are the poor in spirit, for theirs is the kingdom of heaven" (Matt. 5:3). This is the first blessing Jesus articulated in the arrangement known as the Beatitudes. A few readers think about what "poor in spirit" signifies. No doubt it is a difference to pride and ego. People who are proud and self-centered clearly have no place in God's kingdom, while the humble and God-focused will love it.

◇◇◇◇◇

## Blessed Are The Persecuted

As the centuries progressed, one thing has been consistent: Good people have been persecuted. Jesus disclosed to His disciples this would be so. Be that as it may, in the Beatitudes (Matt. 5), Jesus promised that however His people may fall by natural principles (earthly standards), there is a rich reward in the endless plan of things:

"Blessed are those who are persecuted for righteousness

sake, for theirs is the kingdom of heaven. Blessed are you when they revile and persecute you, and say a wide range of evil against you falsely for My sake. Rejoice and be exceedingly glad, for great is your reward in heaven, for so they persecuted the prophets who were before you" (v. 10-12).

◇◇◇◇◇

## Perfect Christians

"Thusly you will be perfect, similarly as your Father in heaven is perfect" (Matt. 5:48). "Be perfect," you state? Incomprehensible, you state? Maybe not. The Bible researchers guarantee us that the word we translate as "perfect" signifies something progressively like "whole."

Unquestionably it doesn't mean perfect in looks and such shallow things. Truth be told. The fact is frequently cited outside of any relevant connection to the issue at hand. What comes just before it are Jesus' words about loving one's adversaries. In the event that we can do that-and the New Testament commands it over and over then we are well while in transit to being perfect, fit for everlasting fellowship with God.

◇◇◇◇◇

## Treasures In Heaven

Jesus clarified that rich individuals experience considerable difficulties entering heaven. He also knew that many individuals, rich or poor, are fixated on cash and natural belongings. "Try not to lay up for yourselves treasures on earth...but lay up for yourselves treasures in paradise, where neither moth nor rust decimates and where thieves don't break in and steal.

For where your fortune is, there your heart will be also" (Matt. 6:19-21). As it were, righteousness perseveres through perpetually, even past the grave, while our natural belongings don't continue (nor do the people who esteem assets regardless of anything else).

◇◇◇◇◇

## The Heavenly Banquet

More than once in the New Testament heaven is contrasted with a terrific meal. Matthew 8 records the gathering of Jesus with a Roman centurion who begs Him to heal his servant. Most Jews disdained the Romans (and the other way around), however Jesus was profoundly inspired with the man's faith.

Jesus said to His followers, "Without a doubt, I say to you, I have not discovered such great faith, not even in Israel! Furthermore, I state to you that many will originate from east and west, and take a seat with Abraham, Isaac, and Jacob in the kingdom of heaven" (vv. 10,11). In this way, heaven will be brimming with surprises. A few people who hope to be there won't be, and the other way around.

◇◇◇◇◇

# Who Is The Greatest!

God does not consider things the way people do-this is a key subject of the Bible. Jesus clarified that "greatness" as man ordinarily characterized it isn't what prompts eternal life. Jesus' followers asked Him, "Who Then is most prominent in the kingdom of heaven?" Jesus at that point called a little child to Him and stated, "Except if you are converted and move toward becoming as little children, you will in no way, shape or form enter the kingdom of heaven.

In this manner whoever humbles himself as this little youngster is the greatest in the kingdom of heaven" (Matt. 18:1-4). "Move toward becoming as little children" does not signify "act like ruined whelps." It alludes to being straightforward, humble, not pleased or self-assertive.

◇◇◇◇◇

# The Great Promise To Nicodemus

John 3:16 is without a doubt a standout amongst the most cited verses of the entire Bible. Individuals regularly overlook its specific circumstance: Nicodemus, a Pharisee, visited Jesus by night and started a dialog of eternal life. It brought about a standout amongst the most significant chapters in the Bible.

Herewith the popular verse and the one that pursues: "God so loved the world that He gave His only begotten Son, that whosoever believeth in Him ought not die but rather have everlasting life. For God did not send His Son into the world to condemn the world, but that the world through Him may be saved" (3:16,17).

◇◇◇◇◇

## Abraham's Bosom

Abraham was profoundly and physically the predecessor of Israel, the "father of the faithful." As Israel started to have faith in a blessed afterlife in the wake of death for the faithful, they normally trusted the godly Abraham would be in heaven. The expression "in Abraham's bosom" (or "at Abraham's side") had the same meaning as "in heaven."

Jesus utilized the expression in His illustration of the rich man and the poor beggar (Luke 16:22,23). The dead beggar Lazarus wound up "in Abraham's bosom" while the rich man was tormented in a fiery hell.

◇◇◇◇◇

## The Parable Of The Lost Sheep

Jesus taught the love for God, but He also instructed that hell is genuine. All things being equal, He clarified that God wanted that everyone would come to Him. Jesus told the story of a shepherd who had one hundred sheep, one of which had strayed into the mountains.

The shepherd left the ninety-nine to search out the stray. "Indeed, even so it isn't the desire of your Father who is in heaven that one of these little ones should perish" (Matt. 18:10-14).

◇◇◇◇◇

## The Sadduccees And The Resurrection

Among the Jews of Jesus' time, the Sadducees were the aristocratic party, common, and responsible for the Jewish ministry (the priesthood). In contrast to most Jews, they didn't accept there would be a resurrection or a heaven. Realizing that Jesus did, they spun Him a strange conundrum about a woman who weds seven brothers in progression, with every one leaving her a widow.

In the afterlife, the Sadducees ask, whose spouse will she be? Jesus saw this absurd enigma for what it was, but He gave a significant answer: "In the resurrection they neither wed nor are given in marriage, but are like the angels of God in heaven" (Matt. 22:30).

At the end of the day, the binds that individuals need to each other on earth won't really apply in heaven. All things considered, in heaven nobody would reproduce, and our most profound relationship will be with God.

◇◇◇◇◇

## The Living Bread

The Old Testament records the tale of the phenomenal nourishment, bread from heaven that sustained the Israelites after their mass migration (exodus) from Egypt. In John's gospel, Jesus spoke about Himself as a far better bread from heaven: "I am the living bread which came down from heaven.

If anyone eats of this bread, he will live forever" (6:51). Though the sustenance was just a transitory "fix" for hunger, Jesus Himself is the eternal bread that fulfills man's most profound hunger.

◇◇◇◇◇

## Losing Life To Save It

"If that anyone desires to come after Me, let him deny himself, and take up his cross day by day, and follow Me. For whoever wants to save his life will lose it, however whoever loses his life for My sake of will save it" (Luke 9:23,24). These expressions of Jesus clarify that Jesus' message was some way or another "unnatural" - for individuals, being childish,selfish commonly, quite often attempt to protect their very own life in this world.

Be that as it may, Jesus had the following next world always in sight (paradise), and those who might enter His kingdom would do likewise.

◇◇◇◇◇

## The Parable Of The Good Samaritan

One of the teachers of the Jewish law asked Jesus, "Teacher, what will I do to inherit eternal life?" Jesus answered by citing the two essential rules: Love God, and love your neighbor. When the teacher ask, "And who is my neighbor?" Jesus answered with the well known illustration of the great Samaritan.

In the story, a man is beaten and victimized and left for dead. The "good" religious Jews cruise him by, but a Samaritan (the Jews and the Samaritans despised one another) stops and gives the man help (Luke 10:25-37).

Jesus had officially expressed that to have eternal life we should love our neighbor, and His story proposes that "love for neighbor" incorporates showing mercy to those who are our enemies.

◇◇◇◇◇

## Forsaking All For God

Being a disciple of Jesus wasn't equivalent to joining a club. His twelve men needed to forfeit a lot to follow Him. Peter said to Jesus, "See, we have left all and followed You." Jesus answered, "Certainly, I say to you, there is no one who has left house or parents or brothers or wife or children, for the sake of the kingdom of God, who shall not receive many times more in this present time, and in the age to come everlasting life" (Luke 18:28-30).

◇◇◇◇◇

## Be Prepared

"Be prepared" is the watchword used by Jesus for the those who seek after eternal life. "Take heed to yourselves, least your hearts be weighed down with carousing, drunkenness, and cares of this life, and that Day come on you unexpectedly...Watch accordingly, and supplicate dependably that you might be counted worthy to escape from every one of these things that will happen, and to stand before the Son of Man" (Luke 21:34, 36).

◇◇◇◇◇

## Aionios

The Greek word is utilized seventy-eight times in the New Testament and is deciphered "eternal" or "everlasting" or "forever." "Eternal life" is the manner by which we interpret zoe aionios. It signifies "life of the age to come," but the New Testament clarifies this isn't only a postdeath experience, but something that Christians start to experience in this life.

◇◇◇◇◇

## This Is Life Eternal

John's gospel more than once alludes to "eternal life," however not at all like the book of Revelation, it gives us no visual portrayal of eternity, (for example, golden avenues, pearly gates, and harps). The book of John tells us some vital things about eternal life, prominently that it includes being close to God. Think about the expressions of Jesus' petition to His Father. "This is everlasting life, that they may know You, the only true God, and Jesus Christ whom You have sent" (17:3).

◇◇◇◇◇

## The Resurrection And The Life

Chapter 11 of John's gospel recounts Jesus' raising His companion Lazarus from the dead. Before He achieved this great miracle, He said to Lazarus' sister Martha, "I am the resurrection and the life. He who believes in Me, though he may die, he shall live" (11:25).

The way that He raised Lazarus is evidence that his words to Martha were not a vain boast. The raising of Lazarus is a kind of "preview" of what will happen for all who trust in Jesus Christ.

◇◇◇◇◇

## Reward For Bearing The Cross

Jesus did not preach a simple message: "If anyone desires to come after Me, let him deny himself, and take up his cross, and follow Me" (Matt. 16:24). Clearly this isn't a message everyone can accept, but there is a payoff in the eternal sense: "The Son of Man will come in the glory of His Father with His angels, and afterwards He will reward each according to his works" (16:27).

For a some people, fellowship with the Father, the Son, and the angels might be worth a life of self-denial.

◇◇◇◇◇

## The Transfiguration

Were the saintly men of the Old Testament already in heaven? The Gospels suggest that this was the case. Consider the event known as the Transfiguration: "Jesus took Peter, James, and John his brother, brought them up on a high mountain by themselves; and He was transfigured before them.

His face shone like the sun, and His clothes became as

white as the light. And behold, Moses and Elijah appeared to them, talking with Him...a bright cloud overshadowed them; and suddenly a voice came out of the cloud, saying, 'This is my beloved Son, in whom I am well pleased. Hear Him!" (Matt. 17:1-3, 5).

In Jewish tradition, Moses represented the Law while Elijah represented the great prophets of Israel. This amazing encounter serves as proof that Moses and Elijah were not just dead-and-buried saints, but also living men.

◇◇◇◇◇

## Many Mansions

"In my Father's home are many mansions: If that it were not so, I would have let you know. I go to set up a place for you. I go and set up a place for you, I will come back again and receive you unto Myself; that where I am, there you might be also" (John 14:2,3).

These expressions of Jesus' to His disciples are clearly alluding to heaven, however exactly what are these "many mansions?"

The Greek word that we decipher "mansions" really signifies "dwellings" or even "rooms." Jesus significance is by all accounts that there is a lot of room in paradise for those with faith to enter there.

It also proposes that there is room for uniqueness in heaven, as the commentator Matthew Henry puts it: "Though all shall be swallowed up in God, yet our individuality will not be lost there," for there are "distinct dwellings, and apartments for each."

◇◇◇◇◇

# My Kingdom Is Not Of This World

Jesus' preliminary (trial) before the Roman governor Pilate is a fascinating showdown: crude earthly natural power confronting a definitive spiritual power. Jesus' foes, planning to be freed of Him, wished to raise Pilate's doubt by having him imagine that Jesus was simply one more Jewish revolutionary, another "king of the Jews."

They realized that Pilate would rapidly execute such an person. However, Jesus truthfully assured Pilate, "My kingdom isn't of this world. If my kingdom were of this world, My servants would fight, so I should be delivered to the Jews; yet now My kingdom isn't from here" (John 18:36). Indeed, even as he grudgingly consented to Jesus' crucifixion, Pilate knew that this Jesus was no danger to him or to Rome.

◇◇◇◇◇

# Today In Paradise

The Gospels reveal to us that Jesus was killed between two crooks, one of whom mocked Him as he was dying. Be that as it may, the other one, seeing eternity before him, said to Jesus,"Lord, remember me when You come into Your kingdom." Jesus answered, "Definitely, I state to you, today you will be with Me in Heaven" (Luke 23:30-43).

So the last person Jesus addressed before his dying was a humble criminal. Custom names the apologetic hoodlum Dismas, and Christians point to his very late change as the exemplary case of a deathbed repentance.

Afterward, Christian authors worked to accommodate the "today" of Jesus' words with the New Testament instructing that the last fate in heaven lies in the future. A few authors clarified that heaven alludes not to heaven itself but rather to a happy state where the saved person waits for the Last Judgment, after which he will go to heaven.

◇◇◇◇◇

## Jesus Or The Gardener

On Easter morning, Jesus' committed follower Mary Magdalene went to the Lord's tomb and thought that it was vacant, with two angels inside. Thinking about where Jesus' body had been taken, she heard a man ask here, "Woman, why are you weeping? Whom are you seeking?" Mary assumed the man was the gardener, and she asked him where Jesus' body was. "Jesus said to her, "Mary!" She turned and said to Him, 'Rabboni!' (or, in other words, Teacher)" (John 20:11-16).

Unmistakably, Mary did not perceive Jesus' physical appearance at first, however maybe the commonplace tone of His voice worked. It bears repeating: Jesus' resurrection body was a new form of His earthly body-similar, yet not the same.

◇◇◇◇◇

## The Road To Emmaus

One thing is obvious from the Gospels: After Jesus was raised from the dead, His body was not the same as (but still similar to) His earthly body. Luke's gospel records the story of two of His followers advancing from Jerusalem to a town called Emmaus.

While walking and talking together, they were joined by a third man, whom they didn't promptly perceive as their Master. He participated in their exchange of the ongoing occasions (His own torturous killing (crucifixion and resurrection), but they didn't remember Him until the point when He went along with them at a dinner in Emmaus.

"At that point their eyes were opened and they knew Him; and He vanished from their sight. Also, they said to each other, 'Did not our heart consume inside us while He chatted with us out and about, and keeping in mind that He opened the Scriptures to us?" (Luke 24:31,32). Unmistakably, this was the Jesus they had known, but sufficiently extraordinary that they didn't remember Him amid their long walk to Emmaus.

◇◇◇◇◇

## They Had Seen A Spirit

Gathered in Jerusalem, Jesus' disciples were examining the story that He had been resurrected. "Presently as they said these things, Jesus Himself stood amidst them, and said to them, 'Peace to you.' But they were unnerved and alarmed, and assumed they had seen a spirit.

He said to them, 'For what reason would you say you are disturbed? For what reason do questions emerge in your souls? See My hands and my feet, that it is I Myself.

Handle Me and see, for a soul does not have fragile living flesh and bones as you see I have."

And when despite everything they questioned, He ate some fish and some honeycomb as an approach to show that He might have been, in fact, raised bodily, not similarly as apparition or phantom (Luke 24:36-43).

Unmistakably the resurrected body (the "spiritual body," as Paul called it) is like, yet unique in relation to, the earthly body.

◇◇◇◇◇

## Doubting Thomas

The expression "doubting Thomas" has progressed toward becoming piece of our dialect. Thomas was one of Jesus' twelve disciples, one who happened to be far from the gathering when the resurrected Jesus appeared to them. The others revealed to him they had seen the risen Jesus, yet Thomas was suspicious.

"Except if I find in His hand the print of the nails, and put my finger into the print of the nails, and put my hand into His side, I won't believe." Then eight days after the fact, every one of the followers, including Thomas, were assembled, and "Jesus came, the doors being closed, and stood in the midst."

He was mindful of Thomas' questions, and He said to him, "Reach your finger here, and take a look at My hands; and reach your hand here, and place it into My side. Try not to be unbelieving, however believing." Thomas was then persuaded (John 20:24-28).

This story is fascinating for a few reasons: For one,

Jesus some way or another showed up in the room even with "the doors being closed." Was His resurrected body ready to go through shut doors? John's gospel had officially revealed that the risen Jesus was at first not perceived by Mary Magdalene (John 20:11-16), so unmistakably He was changed somehow.

However unmistakably the injuries from the Crucifixion were as yet noticeable, for He showed these to Thomas.

◇◇◇◇◇

# The Ascension

Every one of the four Gospels report that Jesus became alive (resurrected) once again and appeared to His followers a while later. Just Luke reports what happened to Him after that: "Presently it happened, while He blessed them, that He was separated from them and carried up into heaven" (Luke 24:51).

In Acts 1:10,11, he adds more detail to this record: "While they looked unfalteringly toward heaven as He went up, observe, two men remained by them in white clothing, who likewise stated, "Men of Galilee, for what reason do you stand looking up into heaven?

This same Jesus, who was taken up from you into heaven, will so come in like way as you saw Him go into heaven." This is known as the Ascension, and it is referenced a few times in the New Testament. The early Christians trusted that, similarly as Jesus had left the earth to climb to heaven, He would before long come back from heaven and take His followers home.

# CHAPTER

# THIRTEEN

◇◇◇◇◇

# What The Apostles Taught

◇◇◇◇◇

## The Right Hand Of God

A few times the Bible alludes to Jesus, after His ascension into heaven, as being at "the right hand of God" (Acts 2:33; 5:31; 7:55; Rom. 8:34; Eph. 1:20; Col. 3:1; Heb. 1:3; 12:2; I Pet.3:22). Since God does not have a literal right hand, What does this mean? In Bible occasions, similarly as today, the "right hand man" was special. To sit at a host's right hand at a dinner was to have the place of honor.

"The right hand of God" implies that Jesus is next to God Himself in honor.

◇◇◇◇◇

## The Sadducee - Pharisee Ruckus

Paul the apostle ended up in a bad position ordinarily, as the book of Acts lets us know. On one event, hauled before the Jewish decision gathering (Jewish Council), he cleverly figured out how to transform his preliminary into a fight. "At the point when Paul saw that one section were Sadducees and alternate Pharisees, he shouted out in the board, 'Men and brethren, I am a Pharisee, the child of a Pharisee; concerning the hope and resurrection of the dead I am being judged!"

Also, when he had said this, a discord emerged between

the Pharisees and the Sadducees; and the get together was divided. For the Sadducees state that there is no resurrection and no angel or spirit; but the Pharisees admit both" (Acts 23:6-8).

In the resulting fight, the Roman authorities removed Paul, dreading he would be shredded. Paul saved his skin by proclaiming that he believed in the afterlife.

◇◇◇◇◇

# From Darkness To Light

Called to defend himself before the Jewish official Agrippa, Paul displayed basically a mind-blowing story and transformation to Christianity. He revealed to Agrippa that he received specifically from the Lord his commission "to open their eyes and to divert them from darkness to light, and from the power of Satan to God" (Acts 26:18).

Paul himself had been blinded by his vision of Jesus, so there was an uncommon importance when he spoke about abandoning darkness to light. Ordinarily in the Bible the works of Satan and the works of God are contrasted with darkness and light.

◇◇◇◇◇

# Joint Heirs

The Bible instructs that Christ, as the Son of God, is beneficiary (heir) to all-that is, He will govern God's domains and is the main inheritor of heaven. Romans 8

125

reveals to us that similarly as Christ called God "Father," so can we, for we are spiritually adopted by God.

We become His children, "and if children, beneficiaries (heirs) of God and (joint heirs) beneficiaries with Christ, if for indeed we suffer with Him, that we may likewise be glorified together" (vv.14-17).

◇◇◇◇◇

## Whether We Live Or Die

The early Christians had a certain faith in heaven, to such an extent that heaven appeared as genuine (or all the more so) as earth itself. Paul, in Romans, reminds Christians that they are the Lord's, both in this world and the following. "For if we live, we live to the Lord; and if we die, we die to the Lord. Hence, regardless of whether we live or die, we are the Lord's (14:8).

◇◇◇◇◇

## Eye hath Not Seen

"Eye hath not seen, nor ear heard, neither have gone into the heart of man, the things which God hath prepared for them that love him" (I Cor.2:9). In these words the apostle Paul talked about the wonderment of eternity, Which must be depicted as indescribable.

◇◇◇◇◇

## An Imperishable Crown

The word we decipher as "crown" for the most part alluded to the shrub wreath put on the heads of victors in athletic challenges. Paul utilized the representation of such rivalries when he talked about running a race with a perpetual crown as the prize. At the end of the day, the best prize of all isn't a crown of leaves (which will shrink, as will earthly glory), however the Great prize itself, eternal life (I Cor. 9:25).

◇◇◇◇◇

## Hope

The word is utilized in the typical sense in the Bible, but it likewise had some more profound implications. In the Old Testament, Israel's incomparable hope was that God would at last deliver the country from all political abuse and the people would experience the heavenly lives God expected of them.

In the New Testament, the key seek is after eternal life. This isn't only a desire or dream, but an articulation, in view of the promises of Christ. Paul stressed that despite the fact that faith in Christ brought fulfillment in this earthly life, significantly increasingly essential was what lay ahead: "If in this life just we have hope in Christ, we are of all men the most pitiable" (I Cor. 15:19).

◇◇◇◇◇

# As In Adam All Die

Our to a great degree sensational area of Handel's Messiah is the melodic setting of the words, "As in Adam all die, even so in Christ will be made alive" (I Cor. 15:22). The "Adam" segment is low and melancholy, but the "Christ" section is noisy and triumphant, as though Handel were setting the resurrection to music.

Paul's words have been confused, misinterpreted: "In Christ all will be made alive" does not allude to the whole human race, but rather to Christians, which is clear if you read all of I Corinthians 15. The resurrection and heaven are not for all, for all won't put their faith in Jesus Christ.

◇◇◇◇◇

# The Last Enemy

"The last adversary (enemy) that will be crushed is death" (I Cor. 15:26). In his acclaimed section on the raising of believers to everlasting life, Paul guaranteed that death will at long last be devastated until the end of time. While Christians will at present need to confront physical death, death has no extreme power, for just as Jesus Christ rose again after His death, so will all believers do so.

◇◇◇◇◇

# Eat And Drink, And Nothing More

Paul stressed over and over that Christ had become alive once again, thus would all who trusted in Him. If that this isn't thus, he stated, Christianity is useless, meaningless. "If the dead don't rise, 'Let us eat and drink, for tomorrow we die!" (Cor. 15:32).

As such, if this earthlyl life is all we have, why mess with profound morality or faith, since the best thing is to enjoy our yearn for pleasure. But, Paul insisted that there is an actual existence (afterlife, heaven, eternal life) after this this life.

◇◇◇◇◇

# The Spiritual Body

This expression sounds conflicting, even contradictory: How can a body be "spiritual" (non-material), for a body must be material? Paul may have known that this expression sounded silly, but it was the main method for portraying something incredible: the body of Christians after they are resurrected.

Jesus, raised from the dead, set the example, and the Gospels demonstrate that His risen body was like - but in also unique in relation to (or different from) - His earthly body. Paul reveals to us that similarly as our earthly bodies are like the body of Adam, so our risen bodies will be like the body of the risen Christ. Our earthly body is dust, our new body is heavenly (I Cor. 15:35-48).

◇◇◇◇◇

## In The Twinkling Of An Eye

"Behold, I reveal to you a mystery: We will not all sleep, but rather we shall be changed-in a moment, in the twinkling of an eye, at the last trumpet. For the trumpet will sound, and the dead will be raised incorruptible, and we will be changed (transformed)" (I Cor. 15:51,52). Awesome words, right?

Presently wonder these words, set to music, are so wonderful a piece of Handel's Messiah. Paul, with regards to Jewish tradition, trusted that an impact of the trumpet would flag the resurrection of the righteous. (He didn't make reference to a heavenly attendant blowing the trumpet, but that is the customary view).

The fact that Paul spoke of "we" shows that he himself would have liked to be alive on earth when the trumpet sounded.

◇◇◇◇◇

## O Death, Where Is Thy Sting?

"O death, where is thy sting? O grave, where is thy victory?" So wrote Paul in I Corinthians 15:55, near the end of his glorious and triumphant chapter about the resurrection of the dead. He was re-accentuating that Christ had crushed, defeated man's last enemy, death, and that death and the grave need never again fill us with fear.

The refrain has for quite some time been a piece of the Anglican (Episcopalian) internment benefit and has gone into basic use in English. It was also set to music in Handel's Messiah.

◇◇◇◇◇

## From Glory To Glory

Paul discussed the "unveiling" of the Word of God. Paul, raised an ardent Jew, came to see, after his change to Christianity, that there is a shroud (veil) (spiritually speaking) over the Jews' hearts, a veil that by one way or another isolates or separates them from God.

With Christians there is no veil: "We all, with unveiled face, beholding as in a mirror the glory of the Lord, are being transformed into the same image from glory to glory" (II Cor. 3:18).

In the Old Testament, Moses alone observed God face to face. In the New Testament, on account of Christ, all believers may draw close to God. Paul suggested that we won't need to wait that heaven for this to occur, for it begins now in our own lives.

◇◇◇◇◇

## The Weight Of Glory

Life in this world isn't always easy, and Christians bear the weight of here and there being mistreated for their faith. Paul had a few encouraging statements: "Our light affliction, which is but for a moment, is working for us a far more exceeding and eternal weight of glory...For the things which are seen are temporary, but the things which are not seen are eternal" (II Cor. 4:17,18).

In the great scheme of things, our afflictions on earth, regardless of how difficult (burdensome), are "light," while time eternity has "weight," for it endures.

◇◇◇◇◇

## Tent vs House

Before they had the temple as a place of worship, the Israelites fixated their worship on the tabernacle, an expansive tent. So the tabernacle was just transitory, while the temple was intended to be permanent. Paul had this as a primary concern when he revealed to Christians that our earthly bodies are just "tents," while we have "a building from God, a house not made with hands, eternal in the heavens." While we endure burdens in our earthly "tents," we can look forward to a heavenly home that endures (II Cor. 5:1-8).

◇◇◇◇◇

## Out-Of-Body Experiences

Paul depicted a mysterious Christian (maybe himself) who had been made up for lost time in the "third heaven... whether in the body or out of the body I do not know" (II Cor. 12:2,3). While Paul is by all accounts portraying a vision of heaven, a few Christians today have professed to have out-of-body experiences like Paul's.

Some would call such individuals "the insane person

periphery," however others may state that if Paul had such an event, couldn't Christians today?

◇◇◇◇◇

# Paradise

We use it as an equivalent word for "paradise," and that is the way the Bible uses it. Jesus on the cross promised the repentant thief crucified near Him, "I say to you, today you will be with Me in Paradise" (Luke 23:43). Paul in II Corinthians 12:4, talks about a man (himself, clearly) who was gotten up to speed to heaven and who heard inexpressible things.

Paul, it appears, had a look at paradise. Revelation 2:7 mentions "the tree of life, which is amidst the Paradise of God." The word is from the Greek paradeisus, signifying "parkland."

◇◇◇◇◇

# Sowing To The Spirit

The flesh itself isn't shrewd (evil) (since God made it), however Paul regularly utilized the expression "the flesh" to allude to the life of joy chasing, living as though this material world is everything that matters.

He differentiated the life of the flesh with the life of the Spirit, and guaranteed that "he who sows to the flesh will of the flesh reap corruption, but he who sows to the Spirit will of the Spirit reap everlasting life" (Gal. 6:8).

# CHAPTER

# FOURTEEN

◇◇◇◇◇

## Heavenly Places

Paul utilized "heavenly places" five times in his letter to the Ephesians, and these are the only times it happens in the Bible. He expressed that God has "raised us up together, and made us to sit together in the heavenly places in Christ Jesus" (Eph. 2:6). (See likewise Eph. 1:3; 1:20; 3:10; 6:12).

◇◇◇◇◇

## Saint

The Catholic church characterizes a holy person as an individual who is in heaven - made official by a church procedure called "canonization." But the New Testament applies "saint" to all believers, people called to be God's holy ones while living in the sinful world.

Some saints are more "saintly" than others, but all believers whose lives are driven (led) by the Spirit are bound for eternal life. The New Testament epistles made it clear that saints must be reminded that they belonged God and their lives should show it (Eph. 4:1; Col. 1:10; II Cor. 8:4).

◇◇◇◇◇

## Bowing At The Name

Christianity, following the words of Jesus Himself, has constantly made a virtue of humility. Paul's letter to the Philippians is loaded with acclaim for Jesus, the "Divine

One" who humbled Himself, became fully human, and suffered death on the cross.

"Therefore God also has highly exalted Him and given Him the name which is above each name, that at the name of Jesus every knee should bow, of those in paradise, and of those on earth, and of those under the earth" (Phil. 2:9,10). To put it plainly, every being in paradise and on earth and under it (commentators differ on what "under it" signifies) pays homage to Christ as Lord of all.

◇◇◇◇◇

## Conversation In Heaven

"Conversation" to us just signifies "talk," however when the King James Version of the Bible was being readied it could have signified "citizenship" or "commonwealth" (as more current interpretations have it). Paul told the Philippian Christians that "our conversation is in heaven; from whence also we look for the Savior, the Lord Jesus Christ" (Phil. 3:20). At the end of the day, we are already citizens of paradise, even before we die.

◇◇◇◇◇

## Fight The Good Fight

This phrase is a piece of our dialect, notwithstanding for individuals who have no clue it originates from the Bible. Paul prompted his protege, the youthful pastor Timothy, to "fight the good fight of faith, lay hold on eternal life" (I Tim. 6:12).

Earlier in this letter, Paul advised Timothy to "wage the good warfare" (1:18). There is an curious thing about what the Bible tells us concerning heaven: We receive it as the generous, gracious gift of God, but we likewise take an active part in taking hold of it, fighting for it, and working for it.

◇◇◇◇◇

## If We Endure

The life of faith is simple (we have God as our guide and shield) and hard (we confront persecution and weariness). The life of faith isn't for the lazy, nor for slackers. The New Testament reminds us much of the time that we should "go the distance" if we want eternal life. In Paul's words, "If we endure, we will also reign with Him. In the event that we deny Him, He also will deny us" (II Tim. 2:12).

◇◇◇◇◇

## Preserved For Heaven

Poor Paul! In his busy life as an apostle, he made numerous companions, but in addition numerous foes, and on occasion he was even deserted by those he thought were individual believers. He suffered much, but was constantly supported by the conviction that something better was ahead: "The Lord will deliver me from each evil work and save me for His heavenly kingdom" (II Tim. 4:18).

◇◇◇◇◇

# A High Priest In Heaven

The Jews had a high priest who once a year entered the Holy of Holies in the temple and made atonement for the general population's sin. The letter to the Hebrews discloses to us that Someone more prominent has come: We presently have a High Priest in heaven, Jesus, One who is making atonement for our sins eternally. We no longer need of the earthly high priest as the mediator between us and God, for Jesus assumes the role of Mediator forever (Heb. 4:14; 8:1; 9:12).

◇◇◇◇◇

# The Author Of Salvation

The letter to the Hebrews regularly helps us to remember the contrast between the eternal and the transitory. It discloses to us that Jesus is currently our eternal High Priest in heaven, so we never again have need of an earthly priest. As indicated by Hebrews 5:9, Jesus, "having been perfected, He became the author of eternal salvation to all who obey Him." Note the wording: Eternity is for the those who obey.

◇◇◇◇◇

# The Copy And Shadow

This material world we live in appears to be greatly genuine to us, but the letter to the Hebrews flips around this view: It is heaven, and the magnificent heavenly things, that are really genuine (since they continue everlastingly, while what we see around us won't persevere).

As indicated by Hebrews 8:5, the Jewish system of priests and sacrifices is only "the copy and shadow of the magnificent heavenly things." The eternal High Priest, Jesus, is the "model" for the transitory priesthood on earth.

◇◇◇◇◇

## A Better Country

The place that is known for God's promise was, in the Old Testament, Canaan. In any case, in the New Testament is the new promise, heaven, which the book of Hebrews calls a "better" country, the "heavenly country" (11:16).

◇◇◇◇◇

## Cloud Of Witnesses

Chapter 11 of the letter to the Hebrews is known as the "Faith Hall of Fame," applauding the extraordinary saints of faith from the Bible. Chapter 12 distinguishes these as a nephos marturon, "a cloud of witnesses": "Since we are encompassed by so incredible a cloud of witnesses, let us dismiss each weight, and the sin which so effortlessly catches us, and let us keep running with perseverance the race that is set before us" (v. 1).

It seems as though our antecedents in faith are watching us in an infinite open air theater as we "run the race" of a faithful life. Something other than onlookers, they are "witnesses" and good examples for us. This is one of couple of passages in the Bible that recommend that the holy people in heaven are aware, or even participating in, the lives of the holy people (saints) still on earth.

◇◇◇◇◇

## A Kingdom Which Cannot Be Shaken

The investigation of history makes us careful about putting our faith in countries or government officials, for an undeniable reason. They don't persevere. On the other hand, the letter to the Hebrews asserts that God's people "are receiving a kingdom which can not be shaken" (12:28).

In this existence where even the mightiest countries have fallen and disintegrated, this promise should give us fearlessness (courage).

◇◇◇◇◇

## The Best Inheritance

The New Testament frequently contrasts eternal treasure from the useless fortunes we seek after on earth. For the those who have faith in Jesus Christ, there is "an inheritance incorruptible and undefiled and that does not fade away, reserved in heaven for you" (I Pet. 1:4).

◇◇◇◇◇

## Sojourners And Pilgrims

While the righteous people of the Old Testament looked to Canaan as their promised land, their legacy from God, Christians moved their concentration to heaven, something more persevering than Canaan.

Several New Testament passages remind Christians that this world isn't our actual home. In I Peter 2:11, believers are designated "sojourners and pilgrims" - that is, individuals simply "going through" on their way to a superior place.

◇◇◇◇◇

## Partakers Of The Divine Nature

In II Peter we locate an inquisitive promise to Christians: They will move toward becoming "partakers of the divine nature" (1:4). This thought (if not the exact words) manifests a few times in the New Testament. We are reminded that paradise is something beyond opportunity from agony and earthly burdens, something other than the everlasting vibe of delight.

It is sharing-sharing in the idea of God Himself, something that human words and pictures can never completely impart. We don't "progress toward becoming God," however in some sense we do "taste divine nature" such that we can't presently understand it.

◇◇◇◇◇

## Love, The Ticket To Eternity

Knowledge does not save us; right convictions don't save us. Believing is useless without love. As indicated by I John 3:14, "We realize that we have gone from death to life, since we love the brethren. He who does not love his brother abides in death." Without generosity and charity, our "faith" is meaningless and we have no hope of heaven.

◇◇◇◇◇

## Assurance

This alludes to the assurance of being saved, the conviction of heaven after death. The New Testament is certain that believers can have assurance. Paul talked regularly of assurance, thus did John in his epistles, where he associated assurance with the working of the Spirit" "By this we know that we abide in Him, and He in us, because He has given us of His Spirit" (I John 4:13).

◇◇◇◇◇

## The Keys of Hades And Of Death

In Revelation 1, John an experience with the risen Christ, brilliant with unearthly whiteness. Christ promised him that He had died but now lives evermore, and has "the keys of Hades and of Death," implying that He has the power over them. By dying and rising once more, Christ is master over hostile forces of death (1:17,18).

◇◇◇◇◇

## Blessed Are The Dead

Revelation contains many encouraging words, including these: "I heard a voice from paradise saying to me, "Write: "Blessed are the dead who die in the Lord from now on." "Yes,' says the Spirit, 'that they may rest from their labors, and their works follow them" (14:13).

In other words, we abandon the battles and pains, while the good things, (for example, limit with respect to giving, for feeling happiness) never end.

◇◇◇◇◇

## The Marriage Supper Of The Lamb

All through the Old Testament, God's people (the country of Israel) are exhibited as the bride of of God, bound together in a covenant. This changes with the New Testament: The "bride" is never again Israel but the fellowship of all Christians. The book of Revelation speaks about a future "marriage supper," a feast where the Lamb (Christ) and His bride (Christians) will celebrate their union (19:9).

Jesus had referred to Himself as the Bridegroom (Matt. 9:15; Mark 2:19,20; Luke 5:34,35), and spoke about a great banquet in the kingdom of paradise (Matt. 8:11). Christians at the "marriage dinner of the Lamb" are both visitors and a marriage partner.

◇◇◇◇◇

# Pearly Gates And Streets Of Gold

People are so acquainted with considering heaven having pearly gates and streets of gold that we wonder, Is that in the Bible? Indeed it is, and part of a portrayal of the New Jerusalem (heaven) in Revelation 21:21: "The twelve gates were twelve pearls: every individual door was of one pearl. What's more, the road of the city was pure gold.

◇◇◇◇◇

# Harps And White Robes

The well known image of heaven is of white-robed individuals playing harps. This picture originates from Revelation 15:2, which portrays the holy people who held harps given to them by God. And the white robes? Note Revelation 7:9: "behold, a great large multitude which no one could number, of all nations, clans (tribes), peoples, and tongues...clothed with white robes."

White robes symbolizes immaculateness (purity), and the harps symbolize the music of peace and harmony.

◇◇◇◇◇

# The Tree Of Life

It existed in the Garden of Eden, and after Adam and Eve ignored God, God was worried that they may eat its fruit "and live everlastingly" (Gen. 3:22). Whatever the tree was (or represented), God banished the couple from Eden for eternity.

In any case, the Tree of Life is referenced again much later, in Revelation's depiction of heaven, the New Jerusalem (22:2). There the faithful are allowed to eat of its fruit.

# BIBLIOGRAPHY

Burke, J. (1860, 1972) Imagine Heaven. Grand Rapids, MI.: Baker Books

Clapperton, J. A. (1924) The Essentials Of Theology. London, UK.: Charles H. Kelly, Epworth Press

Clarke, W. N. (1912) An Outline Of Christian Theology. New York, NY.: Charles Scribner's Sons

Gilmore, J. (1989) Probing Heaven: Key Questions On The Hereafter. Grand Rapids, MI.: Baker Book House

Hewitt, T. (1960) The Epistle To The Hebrews. London, UK.: InterVaristy

Hendriksen, W. (1975) The Bible On the Life Hereafter. Grand Rapids, MI.: Baker Book House

Hodge, A. A. (1860, 1972) Outlines Of Theology. London, UK.: New York, NY.:Banner Of Truth, Thomas Nelson & Sons, Forgotten Books (Used By Permission)

McArthur, J. F. (1996, 2013) The Glory Of Heaven: The Truth About Heaven, Angels, Eternal Life, 2nd Edition. Wheaton, Ill.: Crossway

Miley, J. (2009) Systematic Theology, Vols. 1&II New York, NY.: Eaton & Mains, Hendrickson Publishers

Ralston, T. N. (1851, 2010) Elements Of Divinity. Whitefish, MO.: Kessinger Publishing

Vine, W. E (2003) Vine's Expository Dictionary Of The Old And New Testament Words. Nashville, TN.: Thomas Nelson (Used By Permission)

Wiley, H. O. (1943) Christian Theology, Vol. III. Kansas City, MO.: Beacon Hill Press Of Kansas City

The Holy Bible (2017) The New International Version. Grand Rapids, MI.: Zondervan Corporation (Used By Permission)

The Holy Bible (1964) Authorized King James Version. Chicago, Ill.: J. G. Ferguson

The Holy Bible (1953) The Revised Standard Version. Nashville, TN.: Thomas's Nelson & Sons (Used By Permission)

The Holy Bible (1901) The American Standard Version. Nashville, TN.: Thomas's Nelson (Used By Permission)

The Holy Bible (1959) The Berkelcy Version. Grand Rapids, MI.: Zondervan (Used By Permission)

The New Testament In The Language Of The People (1937, 1949) Chicago, Ill.: Charles B. Williams, Bruce Humphries, Inc., Moody Bible Institute (Used By Permission)

# ABOUT THE AUTHOR

**The Reverend Dr. John Thomas Wylie** is one who has dedicated his life to the work of God's Service, the service of others; and being a powerful witness for the Gospel of Our Lord and Savior Jesus Christ. Dr. Wylie was called into the Gospel Ministry June 1979, whereby in that same year he entered The American Baptist College of the American Baptist Theological Seminary, Nashville, Tennessee.

As a young Seminarian, he read every book available to him that would help him better his understanding of God as well as God's plan of Salvation and the Christian Faith. He made a commitment as a promising student that he would inspire others as God inspires him. He understood early in his ministry that we live in times where people question not only who God is; but whether miracles are real, whether or not man can make a change, and who the enemy is or if the enemy truly exists.

Dr. Wylie carried out his commitment to God, which has been one of excellence which led to his earning his Bachelors of Arts in Bible/Theology/Pastoral Studies. Faithful and obedient to the call of God, he continued to matriculate in his studies earning his Masters of Ministry from Emmanuel Bible College, Nashville, Tennessee &

Emmanuel Bible College, Rossville, Georgia. Still, inspired to please the Lord and do that which is well – pleasing in the Lord's sight, Dr. Wylie recently on March 2006, completed his Masters of Education degree with a concentration in Instructional Technology earned at The American Intercontinental University, Holloman Estates, Illinois. Dr. Wylie also previous to this, earned his Education Specialist Degree from Jones International University, Centennial, Colorado and his Doctorate of Theology from The Holy Trinity College and Seminary, St. Petersburg, Florida.

Dr. Wylie has served in the capacity of pastor at two congregations in Middle Tennessee and Southern Tennessee, as well as served as an

Evangelistic Preacher, Teacher, Chaplain, Christian Educator, and finally a published author, writer of many great inspirational Christian Publications such as his first publication: *"Only One God: Who Is He?" – published August 2002 via formally 1ˢᵗ books library (which is now AuthorHouse Book Publishers located in Bloomington, Indiana & Milton Keynes, United Kingdom)* which caught the attention of **The Atlanta Journal Constitution Newspaper.**

**Dr. Wylie is happily married to Angel G. Wylie, a retired Dekalb Elementary School teacher who loves to work with the very young children and who always encourages her husband to move forward in the Name of Jesus Christ. They have Four children, 11 grand-children and one great-grandson of whom they are very proud. Both Dr. Wylie and Angela Wylie serve as members of the Salem Baptist Church, located in Lilburn, Georgia, where the Reverend Dr. Richard B. Haynes is Senior pastor.**

Dr. Wylie has stated of his wife: "she knows the charm and beauty of sincerity, goodness, and purity through Jesus Christ. Yes, she is a Christian and realizes the true meaning of loveliness as the reflection as her life of holy living gives new meaning, hope, and purpose to that of her husband, her children, others may say of her, "Behold the handmaiden of the Lord." A Servant of Jesus Christ!

Printed in the United States
By Bookmasters